Lambert Farm

PUBLIC ARCHAEOLOGY AND CANINE BURIALS ALONG NARRAGANSETT BAY

Lambert Farm

PUBLIC ARCHAEOLOGY AND CANINE BURIALS ALONG NARRAGANSETT BAY

Jordan E. Kerber
Colgate University

Harcourt Brace College Publishers

Fort Worth   Philadelphia   San Diego   New York   Orlando   Austin   San Antonio
Toronto   Montreal   London   Sydney   Tokyo

Publisher	Christopher P. Klein
Senior Acquisitions Editor	Stephen T. Jordan
Editorial Assistant	Rick Carruth
Project Editor	Arlene Holt
Production Manager	Debra A. Jenkin
Senior Art Director	Don Fujimoto

Cover Image: Photograph by Jordan E. Kerber

ISBN: 0-15-505190-3

Library of Congress Catalog Card Number: 96-78058

Address for Editorial Correspondence: Harcourt Brace College Publishers, 301 Commerce Street, Suite 3700, Fort Worth, TX 76102.

Address for Orders: Harcourt Brace & Company, 6277 Sea Harbor Drive, Orlando, FL 32887-6777. 1-800-782-4479 or 1-800-433-0001 (in Florida).

(Copyright Acknowledgments begin on page 109, which constitutes a continuation of this copyright page.)

Harcourt Brace College Publishers may provide complimentary instructional aids and supplements or supplement packages to those adopters qualified under our adoption policy. Please contact your sales representative for more information. If as an adopter or potential user you receive supplements you do not need, please return them to your sales representative or send them to:

Attn: Returns Department
Troy Warehouse
465 South Lincoln Drive
Troy, MO 63379

Printed in the United States of America

6 7 8 9 0 1 2 3 4 5 067 10 9 8 7 6 5 4 3 2 1

For Pearl and John

ABOUT THE SERIES

These case studies in archaeology are designed to bring students, in beginning and intermediate courses in archaeology, anthropology, history, and related disciplines, insights into the theory, practice, and results of archaeological investigations. They are written by scholars who have had direct experience in archaeological research, whether in the field, laboratory, or library. The authors are also teachers, and in writing their books they have kept the students who will read them foremost in their minds. These books are intended to present a wide range of archaeological topics as case studies in a form and manner that will be more accessible than writings found in articles or books intended for professional audiences, yet at the same time preserve and present the significance of archaeological investigations for all.

ABOUT THE AUTHOR

Jordan Kerber developed an interest in archaeology at a young age. By the time he entered high school in Massachusetts, he knew he wanted to be an archaeologist. In his junior and senior years he formed an archaeology club and joined the Massachusetts Archaeological Society. During this time he participated in two nearby digs: the Fairbanks House (the oldest wooden standing house in the United States, built in 1636) and the Green Hill site (a 7,500-year-old Native American site). Kerber did his undergraduate studies at Haverford College and majored in anthropology at Bryn Mawr College. He completed his graduate training at Brown University by receiving his Ph.D. in 1984. His dissertation focused on the prehistoric archaeology of a coastal area, Potowomut Neck, on the west shore of Narragansett Bay in Rhode Island.

Kerber has been interested in coastal archaeology since completing his field school on Nantucket in 1978. In particular, he has studied and written on the effects of postglacial sea level rise on prehistoric Native American settlement and subsistence based on his research at numerous sites in southern New England. Kerber also has been active in cultural resource management and public education programs in archaeology. He has worked as a contract archaeologist; an archaeological technician for the National Park Service at the Cape Cod National Seashore; a consultant for the Rhode Island Historical Preservation Commission; a preservation planner for the Massachusetts Historical Commission assisting the Massachusetts State Archaeologist; and, between 1988 and 1990, public education coordinator for the Public Archaeology Laboratory, Inc., in Rhode Island. He is a trustee and vice president of the Chenango Chapter of the New York State Archaeological Association and a former trustee of the Massachusetts Archaeological Society.

Kerber has taught at several colleges and universities, including Brown University, Providence College, and the University of Massachusetts at Boston. Most recently, he has been on the faculty at Colgate University in Hamilton, New York, since 1989, where he is Associate Professor of Anthropology and also has served as director of the Native American Studies Program. He is married to Mary Moran, a cultural anthropologist who also teaches at Colgate University. They have a young daughter and an infant son.

ABOUT THIS CASE STUDY

While the topics included in the *Case Studies in Archaeology* series are many, it can truly be said that the present volume perhaps best exemplifies archaeology as it is practiced in the United States today. It provides an accurate description of the highs and lows of field work, in particular.

In reaction to the rip-roaring, grab-the-loot-and-run visions of archaeology presented in *Indiana Jones* films and others of their ilk, introductory classes in archaeology often emphasize the slow, painstaking, methodical thoroughness of problem-oriented, modern fieldwork. But archaeology as tedium can be overstated too. In fact, occasionally, an archaeologist *will* have an experience that resembles a scene, or two, out of an adventure movie. The difference is that such events rarely occur in the lives of people who make the study of the past their careers. The phenomenon is similar to the difference between real detectives and lawyers and those portrayed in television series. The fictional heroes and heroines have an intriguing and exciting adventure every week whereas such cases come along infrequently in the more mundane careers of law enforcement agents.

This is not to say, though, that archaeology is not filled with tension and excitement. It is simply the case that such thrills and chills are produced less by hails of poisoned arrows and swaying rope bridges over bottomless chasms than by the stresses of trying to be a scholar in the modern world. Bulldozers in neutral at the edges of sites, young professors scrambling for scarce grant money, looters tearing up sites, graduate students fighting over research topics, volunteers with sunstroke, and farm dogs with big teeth are the more common producers of anxiety and adventure for professional archaeologists.

Jordan Kerber's discussion of his trials, tribulations, and ultimate success in investigating the Lambert Farm site presented in this Case Study captures what real life archaeology in the late twentieth century is like. How to acquire, mobilize, and effectively use scarce resources is a key component in conducting modern research. Such skills are important whether one excavates pyramids or outhouses because the resources are almost always fewer than what one desires. Kerber demonstrates his resourcefulness in the following pages and duly recognizes the vital role of the many volunteers that made his work so successful. In addition, he provides a fascinating review of the evidence for dogs in New World archaeology and prehistoric culture. The importance of "man's best friend" was critical to the economies, ideology, and very survival of Native Americans, especially in North America. Kerber does an admirable job of reviewing an important but often neglected part of prehistory.

It is thus that I am very pleased to present this new addition to the Case Studies in Archaeology series. It provides interesting and relevant lessons on why and how archaeology is done in the contemporary world.

Jeffrey Quilter
Washington, D.C.

PREFACE

A central goal of this monograph is to provide both the beginning and the advanced student with an authentic and detailed example of archaeological research in northeastern North America that highlights topics in Native American archaeology. The book emphasizes that archaeology is not always done only in exotic countries by college professors. Even in developed areas of the Northeast and elsewhere, anyone can contribute to important archaeological investigations, but only under professional supervision. The reader learns how archaeologists excavated, analyzed, and interpreted various remains from an unusual prehistoric Native American site in Rhode Island, called Lambert Farm, that was threatened by destruction. In order to accomplish this goal, the book is written in nontechnical language but still makes extensive use of detailed information and in-depth reconstruction of the site's age, its patterns of material remains, subsistence of its Native American inhabitants, and other topics.

Archaeological fieldwork at the Lambert Farm site was performed as part of an integrated program of education and research. Nearly 200 members of the general public excavated the site under supervision of archaeologists at the Public Archaeology Laboratory, Inc. (PAL), the organization that sponsored the program. Public participation was the only way the artifacts from Lambert Farm could have been recovered and preserved since the site was endangered by the construction of a housing project, and there were no legal means to protect it. This comes as a surprise to many, especially because the site is listed in the National Register of Historic Places, designating it as one of our country's most important archaeological resources. Nevertheless, the Lambert Farm site has been destroyed as houses and streets exist today where this remarkable site was once buried.

Lambert Farm was intensively excavated between 1988 and 1990. It is among the most thoroughly hand-excavated sites in New England. The public excavators recovered more than 56,000 archaeological specimens, including well-preserved stone tools, pottery, and food remains dating between about 3,000 and 500 years ago. Further, some startling discoveries were made, most notably three dog burials interred in large mounds of shells that were transported about one mile from the coast. Curiously, several deposits at the site contained the remains of dogs that were not placed in burials but instead were eaten and discarded with other food refuse.

In addition to highlighting the process and results of this recent study, the monograph draws on much comparative archaeological and ethnohistorical information on Native American treatment of dogs in northeastern North America and other regions. This wealth of material provides insight into the meaning of the dog remains at Lambert Farm. In the case of the Lambert Farm project, none of the thousands of remains from the site would have been preserved, nor would this monograph have been written, were it not for the work of highly motivated public participants who contributed in the excavation, laboratory processing, and funding of this joint education/research program in archaeology.

ACKNOWLEDGMENTS

The program of archaeological research and public education offered by PAL and conducted at Lambert Farm and the subsequent laboratory processing and analysis represented an innovative and monumental undertaking. Like any project of this magnitude, several individuals, organizations, and funding sources were instrumental to its completion. First of all, if it were not for the vision of PAL, this unique program would not have occurred. In particular, the commitment, support, and patience of Alan Leveillee, codirector of the program and director of educational programs at PAL, and Deborah Cox, president of PAL, provided the momentum and backing necessary to keep the program afloat for three years; as codirector of the program, I deeply appreciate their encouragement.

Although archaeologists are not usually grateful to developers, Arnie Brier and George Pesce of Commercial Realty, Inc., are to be commended for voluntarily allowing archaeological research to be performed on their property at Lambert Farm prior to the completion of their residential project. They also donated the use of a bulldozer to aid in the fieldwork by stripping the plow zone deposit from a small portion of the site. Their generosity provides an important example of a successful partnership between developers and archaeologists in the cultural resource management of a threatened site. The Rhode Island Historical Preservation Commission, specifically Paul Robinson, State Archaeologist, transformed this program from an idea to a reality by calling PAL's attention to the plight of Lambert Farm, by assisting in negotiating the details of the program with the developers, and by somehow figuring out a way to provide funding for the emergency Phase One operation. The support of the Warwick Historical Preservation Commission is also appreciated.

A list of the program's participants and personnel follows, but I would like to single out the following people for their voluntary contribution and unyielding commitment to the program: John Damon, Don Doucette, Chris Benison, Paul Goulet, Erik Stowers, Kelli Ann Costa, and Cornelia Burr. Also, PAL staff assistants Chris Jasparro, Deena Duranleau, Bob Goodby, and Donna Raymond, and Brown University teaching assistant, Mary Ann Larson, provided invaluable help in both the field and lab. To everyone listed later, *especially* the field school and workshop participants, I extend my heartfelt thanks for all their hard work and for their desire to learn. I apologize to anyone inadvertently left off this list. I also would like to thank the following people who performed analyses on the recovered remains: Ruth Greenspan, Tonya Largy, David George, and Bob Goodby. Christine Rossi prepared Figures 1.1, 1.2, 1.3, 2.4, and 5.2; Laura Thode prepared Figures 3.2, 3.3, 3.4, 4.1, 4.2, and 4.8; and Imogene Lim prepared Figure 4.4. Michael Wiant kindly provided the photograph reproduced in Figure 5.4.

Funding to support archaeological research at Lambert Farm between 1988 and 1990, as well as subsequent laboratory processing and analysis and the program's other components, was generously provided by the following: American Association for State and Local History, Brown University Salomon Fund, Colgate University Division of Natural Sciences, Colgate University Research Council, Colgate University Technological Advisory Council, IBM, June Rockwell Levy Foundation, National Endowment for the Humanities, Rhode Island Foundation, Rhode Island Heritage Commission, Rhode Island Historical Preservation Commission, University of Rhode Island Sea Grant College Program, City of Warwick, PAL, and all the field school and workshop participants.

I wish to give a special thanks to Colgate University for its continued support of this work and the preparation of this manuscript and to my colleagues in the

Department of Sociology and Anthropology for providing me with the proper environment necessary to complete this book. I also acknowledge the assistance of staff of the Colgate University Case Library and the Museum of New Mexico Laboratory of Anthropology Research Library in identifying and tracking down numerous references. I am grateful for the valuable information on prehistoric dog burials from Ashkelon, Weyanoke Old Town, Keatley Creek, White Dog Cave, Grannis Island, and Koster provided by Brian Hesse, Jeffrey Blick, Brian Hayden, John Olsen, David Thompson, and Michael Wiant, respectively. Thanks are also due Michael Glassow for loaning me a copy of his manuscript for *Purisimeño Chumash Prehistory*, which is now published in the Case Studies in Archaeology series. Jeffrey Quilter, Brian Hayden, and Mary Moran read various portions and versions of my manuscript and offered many helpful comments and constructive advice in vastly improving the book.

Finally, I am eternally indebted to my wife, Mary Moran, and my daughter, Pearl, and son, John, both born after fieldwork ended, for allowing me the time away from them to work on this project. Their everlasting support is appreciated in ways that I cannot begin to express.

LAMBERT FARM PROGRAM PARTICIPANTS, ASSISTANTS, AND VOLUNTEERS

Program Codirectors: Jordan Kerber and Alan Leveillee
Public Archaeology Laboratory, Inc., Staff Assistants: Chris Jasparro, Deena Duranleau, Donna Raymond, Bob Goodby, Bill Begley, and Sara Greene
Volunteer Assistants: John Damon, Don Doucette, Erik Stowers, Chris Benison, Kelli Ann Costa, Paul Goulet, and Cornelia Burr
Public Archaeology Laboratory, Inc., Staff Field Crew (Phase One): Jordan Kerber, Alan Leveillee, Bob Goodby, Mary Lynn Rainey, Burr Harrison, Liz Holstein, and Adam Smith
Volunteer Field Crew: Jordan Kerber, Alan Leveillee, Ann Davin, Bob Goodby, Mary Lynne Rainey, Chris Jasparro, Donna Raymond, Ruth Greenspan, Ron Dalton, Denise Mowchan, Lisa Smolski, John Damon, Don Doucette, Robin Lis, Gary Snyder, Nancy Peterson, Mary Moran, Edward Goody, John McNiff, Patricia Millar, Constance Mussells, Cornelia Burr, John Ho, Adam Smith, Elizabeth Eller, Brendan Daly, and David and Benjamin Leveillee
Field School Participants: Chris Jasparro, Sean Casler, Sally Phillips, Roni Riggins, Charlie Rayhill, Patricia Millar, John Damon, Evone Barlow, Lisa Carpenter, Erik Stowers, Brendan Daly, Jan Mauro, Susan Allen, Karen Rafferty, Julie Goulet, Eleanor Earle, Kelli Ann Costa, Robin Lis, Gary Snyder, Don Doucette, Nancy Peterson, Marcos Paiva, Paula Welch, Deb Teixeira, Tom Shannon, Maureen Mulvany, Deena Duranleau, Donna Souza, Paul Goulet, Jennifer Tamburro, Chris Benison, Deb Talan, Nancy Burkholder, Emily Marotti, Paul Tickner, Tucker Densley, Debbie Shamoon, Adrienne O'Connor, Sarah James, Susan Snyder, Heath Cleaveland, Lance Hopenwasser, and Cecilia Carreiro
Weekend Workshops Participants: Don Doucette, Kelli Ann Costa, Cornelia Burr, Constance Mussells, Bob Crook, Paul Goulet, Gilbert Burnett, Margot Grosvenor, Mark Cournoyer, Nancy LeBlanc, Tammy Fortin, Deena and Charles Duranleau, Michael Benedetti, Madeline Champagne, Deborah Craft, Dean Gendron, Jean Hovey, Betty King, Lea Pearson, Richard Prescott, Thomas Radican, Susan Sikes, Josi Spitzer, Wendy Jencks, Maria Rix, Angela and George Camparone, Paul Carcieri, Matt Szenher, Sarah Stevens, Alexander Vezeridis, Terry Van Heusen, Robert Lev, Brian Schwegler, Melinda Hill, and Marjorie Andrews

School Workshops: Western Hills Jr. High School (Teachers: Tom Raspallo, Ed Blamires, and Herb Zakrinson), Winman Jr. High School (Teacher: Janice Place), Wheeler School (Teacher: Alan Leveillee), Guiteras School (Teacher: Betsy Ose), Slater Jr. High School (Teacher: Jean Dixon), Colt School (Teacher: Betsy Ose), and Brown University Learning Community (Junior Scientists Program)

Brown University Field Methods in Archaeology (Anthropology 160): Jordan Kerber (Professor), Mary Ann Larson (Teaching Assistant), Robert Goodby (Field and Lab Assistant), Kil Do Choi, David Conrad, Elizabeth Eller, John Ho, Bryan Mark, Lee Marshall, Janice Murabayashi, Edwin Pendleton, Adam Smith, Georgie Stanley, Noah Tratt, Justin Twaddel, and Nicola Winn

Colgate University Cataloguers: Paul Tickner, Kristin Roy, Nicole Flavin, Lance Hopenwasser, Sascha Goluboff, Greg Winston, Nat Olsson, Jenna Siracusa, Tammy Bailey, Megan Condit, Tara Mahoney, and Kerry Neville

Contents

1 INTRODUCTION   1
The Archaeological Record   2
Coastal Archaeology in the Northeast   4
Site Location, Discovery, and History of Research   8
Site Destruction and Integration of Research and Education   9

2 FIELDWORK   15
Public Participation and Scheduling   15
Sampling Strategy   18
Excavation Procedures   22
Phases One and Two and Unusual Sample Units   26

3 LABORATORY PROCESSING, ANALYSIS, AND INTERPRETATIONS   29
Laboratory Processing   29
Age of the Site   31
Patterns of Prehistoric Artifacts and Chipping Debris   38
Subsistence and Seasonality   51

4 DISCOVERIES   63
Unusual Finds   63
Shell Features   65
The Dog Burials   66

5 NATIVE AMERICAN TREATMENT OF DOGS: LAMBERT FARM IN
    GLOBAL PERSPECTIVE   79
Ancestry of Dogs   79
Archaeological Evidence of Dog Burials and Sacrifices around the World   84
Ethnohistorical Information   94

6 CONCLUSION   103

REFERENCES   109

CHAPTER I

Introduction

This monograph discusses archaeological research conducted at a prehistoric Native American site in northeastern North America that was occupied between about 3,000 and 500 years ago. During those 2,500 years, the site, now known as Lambert Farm and located in Rhode Island, witnessed many episodes of settlement and abandonment by different groups of people—some camped there for several months at a time, and others visited for only a few days. All of the Native American settlers of Lambert Farm are believed to be ancestors of Narragansett Indians who still reside in Rhode Island today. It was the Narragansetts who befriended the Puritan dissident Roger Williams in 1636, after he was banished from Massachusetts and sought religious freedom in Rhode Island, the state he founded. The abundant remains recovered from Lambert Farm—more than 56,000 objects, including some intriguing discoveries such as dog burials within below-ground shell mounds—contribute to our understanding of key topics in the archaeology of Native Americans in the Northeast. Also, the Lambert Farm project provides an important model for the recovery of archaeological remains from similarly significant sites threatened by destruction but not protected by historic preservation laws.

Northeastern North America is an enormous area that has no fixed boundaries. Indeed, archaeologists tend to carve up this region in a number of different ways. For the purposes of this book, the Northeast specifically refers to the formerly glaciated Appalachian provinces of both southeastern Canada and northeastern United States. This region today includes New England; the states of New York, New Jersey, and Pennsylvania; the Canadian Maritime provinces; central and southern Quebec; and southeastern Ontario (Figure 1.1). For many thousands of years this was the homeland of countless groups of Native Americans who lived off the land, from the coasts to the uplands, by hunting, gathering, fishing, and farming. More recently, during the some 400 years of European encroachment, many thousands of native people resided in the Northeast. They belonged to a variety of groups that were seriously affected by contact with the European settlers, often in devastating ways through disease, warfare, and loss of land. These peoples included both Algonquian speakers, such as the Micmac and Abenaki of southeastern Canada and northern New England; the Wampanoag, Narragansett, and Pequot of southern New England and the Delaware farther south; and Iroquoian speakers, such as the Huron of southeastern Ontario and the Five Nations Iroquois Confederacy, consisting of the Mohawk, Oneida, Onondaga, Cayuga, and Seneca of New York. Members of these various tribes still live in the Northeast today.

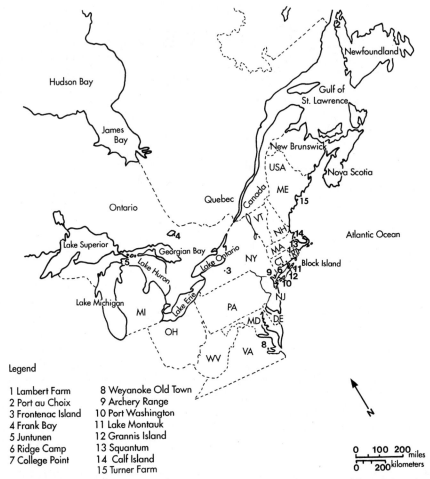

FIGURE 1.1   Northeastern North America and vicinity, showing geographic and site locations mentioned in the text.

Legend

1 Lambert Farm	8 Weyanoke Old Town
2 Port au Choix	9 Archery Range
3 Frontenac Island	10 Port Washington
4 Frank Bay	11 Lake Montauk
5 Juntunen	12 Grannis Island
6 Ridge Camp	13 Squantum
7 College Point	14 Calf Island
	15 Turner Farm

THE ARCHAEOLOGICAL RECORD

One of the goals of any archaeological research project is to reconstruct what life was like for a group of people who lived in the past. Though much archaeology has been done in far away places such as Egypt, Israel, and Mexico, many sites have been excavated across the Northeast in both rural and developed locations. Archaeologists often attempt to answer such questions as, How and where did people live? What major changes in their culture did they experience? What were their settlements like? What did they eat, and how did they obtain and prepare their food? These questions become more difficult to answer when studying nonliterate, prehistoric people such as the Native Americans at Lambert Farm because they did not possess a system of writing to record events. Prehistory, by definition, refers to that time period when written chronicles of events were not kept. On a global scale, this is an extremely long period, accounting for 99% of the time humans have existed. Because documents do not exist for this time period, the primary way to study these ancient people and their cultures is through prehistoric archaeology.

For Native American prehistory in northeastern North America, this period begins with the first human residents of the region (about 12,000 years ago) and lasts until the arrival of Europeans (by 400 years ago for much of the Northeast), who recorded their encounters with various Native American groups. Human prehistory in the Northeast is divided into three major time periods: Paleoindian (ca. 12,000 to 10,000 years ago), Archaic (ca. 10,000 to 3,000 years ago), and Woodland (ca. 3,000 to 500 years ago); both the Archaic and Woodland periods are further separated into early, middle, and late subdivisions. The identification of these periods and subperiods is largely based on determining when important changes occurred in subsistence, settlement, and artifact types, such as projectile points (arrowheads, spear points, etc.).

Nonliterate groups that lived during the prehistoric and historic periods may have recorded important events in the form of stories told by one generation to the next. These oral traditions, however, which continue in many Native American societies today, are not always accurate chronologies of earlier times as they tend to change through embellishment and memory loss over the course of hundreds of years. It is much easier for a historical archaeologist studying people for whom documents exist, such as the Pilgrims of Plymouth Colony or the Iroquois of the eighteenth century, to reconstruct what life was like long ago. But even the documents do not provide a record for everyone in a society or a complete picture of everyday life. That is why historical archaeologists combine what they learn from recovered artifacts with the written record to understand history more completely.

Because archaeologists who study prehistory do not have access to written records of the people in whom they are interested, their research must focus entirely on the remains left by these people, hundreds and even thousands of years ago. It is assumed that the range of objects used by a group and their artifacts, meals, settlements, and so on—which together are known as material culture—reflect the group's behavior and overall culture. Archaeologists often examine certain items at a site that directly reflect specific activities. For example, projectile points provide insight into hunting techniques, while the remains of bones and seeds indicate food preparation and consumption. Thus, some of the common topics explored by prehistoric archaeologists are subsistence, diet, settlement, and technology, since fairly direct evidence of these may be found at sites. On the other hand, other aspects of culture are more difficult to interpret solely from material remains. Ideology or religious belief systems, which were likely central to prehistoric Native American life, may only be indirectly reflected in remains such as human burials and associated grave goods, for instance. Further, not all elements of culture resulted in the use of objects. How does a prehistoric archaeologist study language, kinship, or marriage? These and many other aspects of culture are, at best, extremely difficult to reconstruct in prehistoric societies in which the associated objects, if any, are poorly known.

Another important limitation in our interpretations of prehistory is caused by a bias in preservation. The archaeological record, the repository of archaeological data below and above ground, contains only those material remains that have been preserved. Not all items used by a society survive the ravages of time. Most organic materials, such as bone, wood, and shell, eventually decompose. Rarely are these items preserved in special circumstances such as dry caves, ice, bogs, or even thick shell deposits. Inorganic materials, stone in particular, are preserved much longer, even over millions of years. The most common raw material at the vast majority of prehistoric archaeological sites is stone, not necessarily because it was the most popular material used but because it lasts the longest. Archaeological remains of stone, also called lithics, take the form of chipped-stone tools, such as projectile points, knives, and scrapers; groundstone tools, such as axes and adzes; and chipping debris or flakes, which are the by-products of stone toolmaking. In short, the archaeological record is biased toward the preservation of lithics, and thus stone-tool technology is a common area of study among prehistoric archaeologists.

Consequently, there may be an additional bias in that the archaeological record tends to be more reflective of activities assumed to have been performed by men, such as hunting and stone toolmaking (Gero and Conkey 1991; Spector and Whelan 1989). Among the majority of contemporary and historic hunter-gatherers and horticulturists, women use objects more likely to disappear from the archaeological record, such as baskets, carrying bags, and wooden implements. Pottery, which is commonly produced by women around the world, is one of the few exceptions.

COASTAL ARCHAEOLOGY IN THE NORTHEAST

In the coastal zone of northeastern North America, the archaeological record is biased in yet another important way. The shoreline of the Northeast, as well as around the world, has been in a constant state of flux due to sea level changes following glacial melting. During the Pleistocene period, also called the "Ice Age," much of the earth's northern hemisphere was covered by glaciers. These mountains of ice, some over 1 mile high, formed as a result of colder climates in which snowfall did not melt but accumulated year after year and eventually was compressed into colossal, slowly moving ice sheets. In the Northeast the last glacial advance, called the Wisconsin maximum, occurred near the end of the Pleistocene around 25,000 years ago. During this time, sea level dropped about 400 feet below its present level. Huge areas of dry land, now underwater, were exposed on the continental shelf up to 450 miles east of today's shoreline. Millions of gallons of water from the oceans were locked up as ice in the Wisconsin glacier, which covered the Northeast. During the subsequent Holocene, the glacier melted and receded north. As a result, water returned to the Atlantic Ocean, and sea level began to rise, rapidly at first, flooding the continental shelf. While most of the Northeast's shoreline has been moving progressively inland because of rising sea levels, some of the shoreline is going in opposite directions due to local conditions. For instance, part of the Maine coast is growing, thereby creating an exception to the general rule of sea level rise in the Northeast. In this portion of northern New England, land along the coast, which was once depressed by the enormous weight of the glacier for a longer period than areas farther south, has been slowly rebounding, causing an increase in the size of the landmass and extension of the shoreline into areas once underwater.

Native Americans could not move into southern portions of the Northeast until about 12,000 years ago, after the glacier had retreated from the area and plants and animals could be supported by a warmer climate. These first people in the Northeast, called Paleoindians, remained in the region until about 10,000 years ago. They most likely came from areas to the south and west of the Northeast and were the descendants of the first humans to enter the New World. The first immigrants travelled across a wide stretch of land more than 20,000 years ago. Called the Bering Land Bridge, this stretch of land was able to connect present-day Alaska and Siberia due to lower sea levels. Paleoindians gathered wild plant foods and hunted large game, known as megafauna, that included mastodon, mammoth, and other now-extinct animals. They are well known for the large and finely crafted spear points they used to hunt their prey.

By 12,000 years ago in the Northeast, during the Paleoindian period, sea level was at about 200 feet below its present level, exposing areas on the continental shelf up to about 100 miles east of today's coast. As sea level continues to rise today, it has flooded areas on the continental shelf that may have been inhabited by Paleoindians and other subsequent prehistoric Native Americans. Any archaeological sites that were located there and not washed away by rising sea levels are now in deep water and buried by thick mud deposits. If these sites did survive, it would be extremely difficult for even underwater archaeologists to find them. Thus, the archaeological record in the coastal Northeast is biased against the recovery of prehistoric sites that may have once been situated on the continental shelf.

Because only sites located on dry land today tend to be investigated, understanding patterns of prehistoric coastal adaptation remains a problem. Many archaeologists working in the region note the general absence of dense remains of coastal resources in sites dating to the Paleoindian and the following Archaic periods. It is not until about 4,000 to 3,000 years ago, at the end of the Archaic and the beginning of the subsequent Woodland period, that abundant coastal resources appear in northeastern sites. This pattern leads to contrasting interpretations. On the one hand, one may conclude that Paleoindian and Archaic populations did not intensively use the coastal zone, and that it was primarily later Woodland populations who took advantage of the rich food supply that the coast offered. On the other hand, one could argue that the majority of Paleoindian and Archaic sites that avoided submergence and remain on dry land today were not located near the coast at the time they were being used. Which interpretation is right? Ironically, both may be.

While sea level rise would have flooded ancient sites on the continental shelf, it also contributed to the formation of the coastal zone as an area that would have eventually attracted large settlements. During its initial stages, until about 6,000 years ago, sea level rose rapidly at a rate of more than 5 mm per year. Such a rate contributed to an unstable environment in which coastal resources simply were not plentiful. A notable and rare exception are dense remains of oyster shells from Early Archaic sites dating to as early as 7,000 years ago. These sites are located along the lower Hudson River, just north of New York City, and escaped inundation because of their situation at high elevations above the river. Nevertheless, it was not until between 4,000 and 3,000 years ago, at the end of the Archaic and the beginning of the Woodland periods, that the rate of sea level rise slowed considerably to about 1 mm per year. This decrease enabled the formation of stable and extremely productive coastal ecosystems in the Northeast. Of particular importance to prehistoric Native Americans of the coastal zone was the creation of salt marshes and mud flats that are associated with mature estuaries, coastal bodies of water in which saltwater and freshwater mix daily from the tides. Such an environment and its surrounding land provided lush habitats for a wealth of resources that were exploited by Native American groups—fish, shellfish, waterfowl, and deer. Thus, the lack of abundant coastal resources in Paleoindian and Archaic sites on dry land today is related to both the general absence of conditions that would have supported a rich coastal food supply during these two periods and subsequent inundation of early sites that may have once been situated along former shorelines.

Whatever the reason, it is clear that the most intensive use of the northeastern coastal zone by prehistoric Native Americans occurred during the Woodland period, a time in which several important developments occurred in much of the Northeast. Pottery became widespread, and its production was increasingly refined and elaborated. A greater variety of foods was added to the diet, including, for the first time, domesticated plants such as corn, beans, and squash. Some settlements grew in size and were occupied by many more people, who built large villages in which they lived for at least a year at a time. Also, long-distance trade networks expanded, connecting groups along the coast with those far in the interior. The most common and conspicuous Native American coastal site during the Woodland, or any period in the Northeast, is the shell midden, a deposit that is assumed to be the refuse of prehistoric clambakes. Some middens resemble mounds and contain thousands of shells weighing more than several tons. They represent the accumulation of many meals eaten by small groups of people over several decades, as well as fewer meals eaten by larger groups of people. Other middens are thin scatters of shells discarded in shallow pits and are all that are left of a single meal for a few people. Most shell deposits, however, contain more than just shells. Many contain stone tools and pottery, often broken and thus thrown into the trash, as well as chipping debris, food remains, and other objects. Some organic materials deposited in the midden were preserved by the shell itself. The calcium carbonate in the shells is a strong base material and tends to offset the soil's natural acidity that contributes to decomposition. Thus, as shellfish were highly sought after by prehistoric Native Americans, shell middens are highly prized by coastal archaeologists as they often contain various remains that are rarely preserved in abundance at other sites.

Shell middens are also the subject of debate among northeastern archaeologists. Many of the middens contain the remains of different species of shellfish, often stratified in layers dating between 3,000 and 500 years ago. It is not uncommon to find oysters, mussels, and quahogs in the bottom layers and scallops and softshell clams, dating several hundred years later, toward the top of the same midden. Some researchers have offered explanations for these changes in diet as reflected by the layers of different shellfish species in northeastern middens. One "school," represented by Ritchie (1969) and Snow (1972), believes that the bottom (i.e., oldest) layers of many middens contain primarily shellfish species that were easy to find and catch. They argue that early attempts at shellfish collecting would have focused first on these "easy" species as people were becoming familiar with the coastal environment and its shellfish. The shellfish species distributed toward the top layers were apparently more difficult to find and catch. According to Ritchie and Snow, these species include scallop, which are mobile and required nets to obtain, and softshell clams, which buried themselves deep in mud and were less conspicuous than other species. Thus, they conclude that later in time, as people became more familiar with the coastal environment and its shellfish, their diet shifted to shellfish species that required a more sophisticated technology and intricate knowledge to exploit.

In contrast to this explanation, Braun (1974), among others, has proposed an ecological model. He argues that the different shellfish species distributed in the layers of a midden reflect those species that were available at the time that they were collected. Thus, the shellfish species that were first exploited and whose remains are situated toward the bottom of middens were the ones most available at that particular time. As the coastal environment changed, specifically, water temperature, salinity, and sedimentation, different shellfish species replaced earlier ones as they were better suited to the altered habitats. These new shellfish species were then collected and subsequently deposited in layers closer to the top of the middens. While this model can be tested on the basis of archaeological evidence, other explanations have been put forth that do not readily lend themselves to verification. For instance, Woodland diets may have shifted from one or a few shellfish species to others as a result of changes in taste. It also may be possible that the population of certain shellfish species declined due to overcollecting by Native Americans or from biological contamination ("red tide"). Even prehistoric taboos, including the "Kosher Indian Hypothesis," coined by Newman (1974), have been used to argue for restrictions on eating some shellfish species and not others. A similar argument has been presented to explain the sudden disappearance of fish from the diet of aborigines on northwestern Tasmania around 3,800 years ago (Jones 1978).

At the Lambert Farm site in Rhode Island, the focus of this book, an important discovery reminds us that not all shell middens were simply garbage. While Lambert Farm contained several typical shell middens in which only the remains of meals and other trash were found, the two largest and thickest shell deposits at the site were below-ground mounds that also contained the remains of three domesticated dogs (*Canis familiaris*), carefully buried with associated grave goods. Were these two deposits merely refuse piles, or were they sacred repositories for revered pets, or even sacrificial victims, that were buried with great care? These questions will be addressed later in the book, but it is important to add that the thousands of shells deposited in the two burial mounds were carried uphill at least one mile from the present-day shoreline. It should also be pointed out that both burial mounds contained butchered dog remains discarded as trash. Why were some dogs carefully interred in specially prepared burials, while others were eaten and their remains disposed of at the same site? Insight into this question is also provided later in the book as information is presented on Native American dogs excavated in prehistoric sites and described in historical records of the sixteenth to eighteenth centuries from northeastern North America and other regions. As will be discussed, the evidence indicates that dogs served Native Americans in various and complex ways: as pets, hunting aides, religious sacrifices, emergency and ceremonial food supply, spirit guardians, and afterlife companions.

SITE LOCATION, DISCOVERY,
AND HISTORY OF RESEARCH

Lambert Farm is located in the Cowesett section of the city of Warwick, Kent County, Rhode Island, and is situated approximately 1 mile west of Greenwich Bay on the west side of Narragansett Bay (see Figure 1.2); due to sea level rise, the shore-

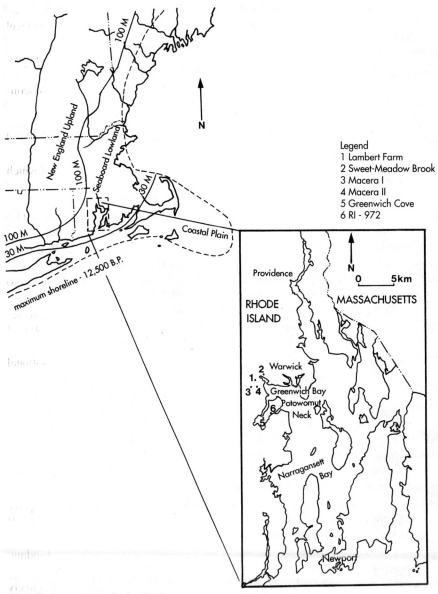

FIGURE 1.2   Narragansett Bay area of Rhode Island, showing the location of Lambert Farm and nearby sites mentioned in the text.

line along Greenwich Bay was slightly farther from the site when it was occupied. Lambert Farm is approximately 800 feet north of the intersection of Cowesett Road and Love Lane and is bounded to the west by a residential development and to the north and east by woodland. The site, as well as all of Warwick, lies within the west-ern portion of the Narragansett Basin, which is located in the Seaboard Lowland section of the New England physiographic province (Figure 1.2). The basin is un-derlain by sandstone, shale, conglomerate, and meta-anthracite coal of the Rhode Island Formation deposited during the Pennsylvanian age about 300 million years ago. Lambert Farm rises in elevation between 90 and 120 feet above mean sea level and sits in a bowllike depression with a steeper, southeast facing slope along its western border. The surficial geology of the site consists of glacial outwash deposits, specifically ground moraine, which is made up of a thin layer of boulders, stone, and other debris carried and deposited by glacial melting at the end of the Wiscon-sin glaciation. These outwash deposits lie above the Pennsylvanian sedimentary bedrock (chiefly shale) and older granite rocks at the site. The vast majority of Lam-bert Farm is situated on well-drained, sandy soil, which is suitable to woodland wildlife habitat. A small area along the southeastern border of the site contains poorly drained soil, associated with a freshwater spring and wetlands, both of which were likely present during the Woodland period when prehistoric Native Americans lived at the site.

The property on which the site was situated had been an active farm owned by the Lambert family since at least 1897. The Lamberts and other artifact collectors recovered archaeological materials from the site over the years. Although it is re-corded in the state site inventory maintained by the Rhode Island Historical Preser-vation Commission, very little was known about Lambert Farm until July 1980 when the first professional archaeological investigation was performed at the site by Morenon (1981). Limited fieldwork involving the excavation of small test pits re-vealed the boundaries of the site to be approximately 2.5 acres (Figure 1.3). Based on this testing, Morenon recovered sufficient information to nominate about 1.8 acres of the site for listing on the National Register of Historic Places. The National Park Service accepted this nomination, and the site was formally listed and thus rec-ognized as one of our country's highly significant archaeological resources.

SITE DESTRUCTION AND INTEGRATION OF RESEARCH AND EDUCATION

Most properties listed on the National Register of Historic Places are buildings, such as Paul Revere's House and Old North Church in Boston. Listing of a property on the National Register, however, does not guarantee legal protection from all forms of disturbance. Historic preservation legislation only protects a National Reg-ister property if it is threatened by a public project—a project that requires funding, permitting, or licensing from a state or federal agency. If a National Register prop-erty is located on private land and is threatened by a private development, it is likely that the property is not protected by any law. Because most of the development in the United States is private, the nation's most important archaeological resources,

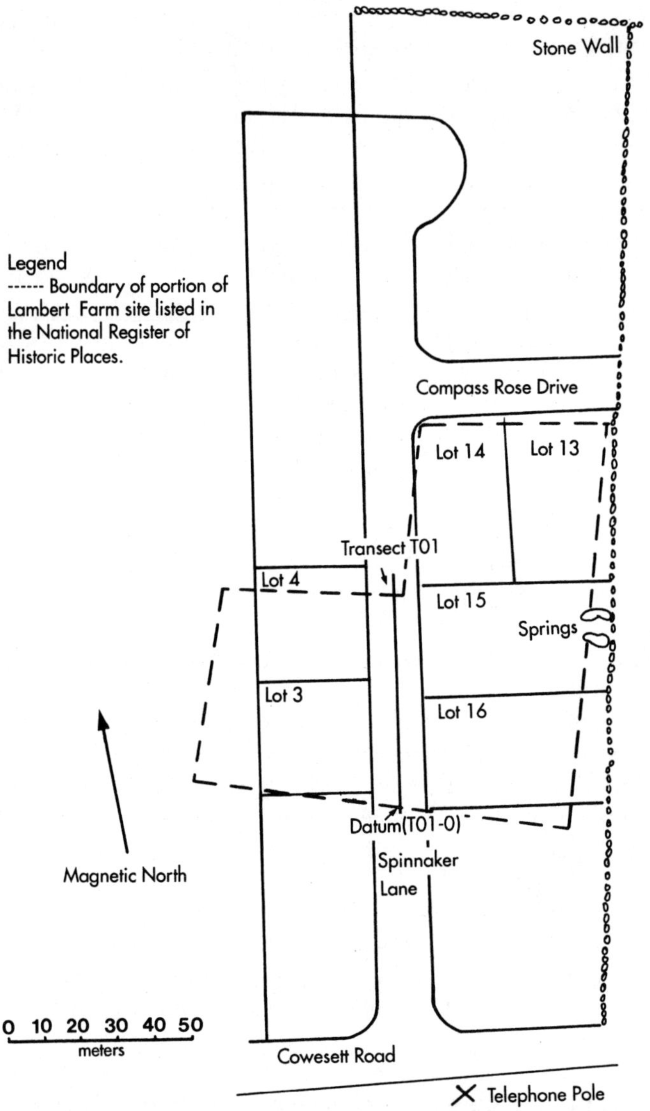

FIGURE 1.3   Proposed residential project plans, showing boundary of portion of the Lambert Farm site listed in the National Register of Historic Places (after Morenon 1981:161).

unfortunately, are at risk of being legally destroyed by shopping malls, condominiums, and countless other private construction projects.

While this comes as a surprise and shock to many, it is sometimes possible to recover the contents of some of these endangered and important sites prior to their destruction. The Lambert Farm case study is one example. Following the 1980 fieldwork performed by Morenon (1981) at Lambert Farm, the property was purchased by two developers who proposed a private residential project consisting of 18 houses and two roads on 10 acres (Figure 1.3). This development threatened the preservation of the entire Lambert Farm site. Since the development was private, the National Register site was not legally protected. Despite community outrage, the developers were free to destroy the site. At the urging of the Rhode Island State Archaeologist, Paul Robinson, a meeting was held in January 1988 at the Rhode Island Historical Preservation Commission in Providence among the developers, the State Archaeologist, and a nonprofit organization dedicated to performing archaeological research and public educational programs, called the Public Archaeology Laboratory (PAL). At the time, I had just begun working at PAL as Public Education Coordinator. I attended the January meeting along with PAL's Director of Public Educational Programs, Alan Leveillee. Both of us sensed that we were about to develop a long-term commitment to the archaeology of the Lambert Farm site based on the developers' unusual sensitivity to our concerns.

Shortly after the meeting, the developers *voluntarily* agreed to delay construction in order to allow archaeological excavation of Lambert Farm. Their cooperation was highly unusual, especially since they were not legally bound to protect the site or to arrange archaeological testing prior to the site's destruction. Based on my previous work experience at the Massachusetts Historical Commission assisting the State Archaeologist, I had seen developers far less cooperative, indeed antagonistic, even when specific historic preservation laws applied to their projects. The Lambert Farm developers decided that between June 1988 and October 1990 they would postpone building six houses (on lots 3, 4, 13, 14, 15, and 16) and for two months delay a road (Spinnaker Lane) within the National Register portion of the site, about 1.8 acres (Figure 1.3). During this 2-year period, PAL in turn agreed to offer a public education/research program in archaeology, which Alan and I co-directed, within the National Register portion of Lambert Farm. A major goal of the project was to recover as much material as possible prior to the site's destruction after October 1990. While the archaeological excavation was in progress, the developers proceeded with bulldozing the land surrounding the Lambert Farm site so that they could avoid further construction delays. The persistent and deafening noise of heavy-duty machinery next to the site while we were digging and recovering artifacts added a considerable amount of stress to our research. It was also a constant reminder of what was soon to happen to all of Lambert Farm. In short, while the developers ultimately destroyed the site following our excavation, they permitted the archaeological recovery of a sizable sample of the remains prior to construction. They could easily have said no to the archaeology at the outset (Figures 1.4, 1.5, and 1.6).

Archaeology, like many things in life, comes with a price. In this situation we had to work hard and fast to raise substantial funding to complete more than just the fieldwork. Once the thousands of artifacts were recovered from the site, they needed to be cleaned, sorted, catalogued, analyzed, reported on, and ultimately stored. All of this required large sums of money. We knew that it was simply not possible to obtain this kind of funding entirely through donations and grants on such a short notice. Also, because the developers were not required by law to preserve the site, they did not offer to pay. In light of these practical constraints created by private development, the direct participation of a varied public in all aspects of archaeological research at Lambert Farm provided the only viable solution to recovering significant

FIGURE 1.4   PAL archaeologists and field school participants at Lambert Farm excavating sample units within area of proposed Spinnaker Lane.

FIGURE 1.5   A few weeks after sampling, field school participants salvage shell features disturbed by the construction of Spinnaker Lane.

FIGURE 1.6   Completion of construction of Spinnaker Lane and lot 4 during the final session of the field school program in August 1990. The remaining portion of the Lambert Farm site that is not yet disturbed by construction is to the right of this photograph.

cultural material that would have been legally destroyed. In addition to funding that we did eventually obtain through numerous grants, a fee was charged to each person who participated in the program at Lambert Farm. Since these funds did not cover all our expenses, PAL provided in-house financial support of the remainder of the program's costs. From the very beginning, both Alan and I were convinced that good, responsible archaeological research could be performed by the public with proper professional supervision and commitment.

Scores of people of various ages and backgrounds participated in the research at Lambert Farm, in either a full- or part-time capacity. Most were involved in one of the several three- or four-week field schools or weekend workshops at the site, while others contributed as part of school and college classes. For most who took part, the chance to work on a dig was a once-in-a-lifetime opportunity. Though nearly all were inexperienced when they started, an enormous amount of work was accomplished. The participants excavated hundreds of test pits and recovered, cleaned, and catalogued thousands of archaeological specimens, which were later analyzed by specialists so that I could write a detailed site report (Kerber 1994a) and ultimately this book. Spin-offs of this unusual program of research and public education were successful at increasing awareness of archaeology and bringing the excavation experience and results to thousands of people who were unable to partic- ipate. Alan and I produced a 25-minute videotape of the program, titled *Back to the Past,* that continues to be seen by many students in schools and colleges. We pre- pared a travelling museum display of recovered artifacts and large photographs and also organized a weekly public lecture series consisting of five talks, both of which were attended by large numbers of people. Lastly, more than 30 in-school talk and slide presentations to all grade levels and numerous newspaper, television, and radio interviews were given by both of us.

In many cases across the Northeast and elsewhere integrated education/research programs in archaeology provide a realistic solution to the problem of site destruction by private development (Kerber 1994b:267). Public field schools and workshops in archaeology, however, do have potential pitfalls, especially if they are conducted simply as glorified "treasure hunts." As argued elsewhere (Kerber 1994b:267–68), I do not propose distributing shovels to as many people as possible and instructing them to excavate sites. Field schools and workshops should not be offered *only* to provide training, recreation, or hands-on experience. Rather, such programs must be conducted within the context of a valid research design, under close supervision by qualified archaeologists, and preferably at sites where destruction is unavoidable.

Other problems that may develop in teaching public field schools and workshops at threatened sites are related to disclosing the specific location of the sites. This increases the potential for vandalism from artifact looters, called pothunters, or from innocent curiosity seekers unaware of the deleterious effects of their digging. Such a risk, however, is moot if the site is going to be adversely affected by construction anyway. Another concern is that overly avid participants on their own may excavate the field school site, or worse, nonendangered sites. While there may be no way to prevent such problems, the likelihood that they will occur can be substantially decreased by stressing the conservation ethic throughout the program. At Lambert Farm, for instance, we did not detect any vandalism, thanks largely to the conscientiousness of the program's participants and the help of interested neighbors who kept a watchful eye on the site "after hours."

These concerns and perhaps others are valid whenever one involves the public at any level in an archaeological dig, even with precautions and safeguards. Despite the potential problems, I firmly believe that the benefits of such programs, both to the public and to archaeology, greatly outweigh the risks. In short, the integration of public education and archaeological research achieved in the Lambert Farm program provides a successful model for cultural resource management in general and the recovery and preservation of data from sites endangered by private development in particular. In the remaining pages of this book, you will explore these and other aspects of the Lambert Farm research and its contribution to Native American archaeology in the Northeast.

CHAPTER 2

Fieldwork

Directing archaeological fieldwork can be physically and emotionally exhausting, even if one does not lift a single shovel. Above all, the director has to remain focused on the project's goals, maintain flexibility to deal with surprising discoveries and unexpected pitfalls, and make sure that everyone involved is constantly doing something constructive. The task is made considerably easier with a well-thought-out research design, a carefully formulated plan to guide the excavation and other phases of the project. Indeed, all professional archaeological fieldwork today is directed by a research design, and the Lambert Farm project was no exception.

One of the critical steps of a research design is the creation of project goals. For the Lambert Farm project, a major goal was to retrieve as much information as possible in the 2 years before the site would be destroyed by residential development. Another goal was to increase public awareness of research methodology, archaeological data, and regional prehistory by providing an opportunity for students, teachers, and others to participate in an authentic archaeological investigation. One of the unusual aspects of the Lambert Farm project that set it apart from many other digs in the Northeast was that the public excavators received on-the-job training through close supervision by professional archaeologists. This was the only way in which an integrated program of research and education in archaeology could succeed. The project simply would not have been possible without active public involvement in fieldwork, laboratory work, and funding.

PUBLIC PARTICIPATION AND SCHEDULING

In order to maximize public participation in the Lambert Farm fieldwork, we needed to offer a variety of ways for people to become involved. In short, we had to meet people's scheduling needs—some, such as high school and college students, had the freedom to participate in the excavation on a full-time basis, while others could only attend part-time because of other commitments. During the 2 years of fieldwork, from June 13, 1988, to August 24, 1990, a total of five field schools and four weekend workshops were taught at Lambert Farm. Organized into three-week and four-week sessions, the field schools were scheduled on weekdays during the summer for six hours per day (Figure 2.1). Several people who could not commit to this schedule were still able to participate in the field schools by attending half-days or fewer than five days per week. Many of the college students who were enrolled full-time

FIGURE 2.1   Field school participants excavating sample units east of Spinnaker Lane construction.

in this education/research program received academic credit from Providence College or Colgate University, providing an additional incentive to participate. Also, 14 students in an archaeological field methods course I taught at Brown University excavated at Lambert Farm twice a week during the 1988 fall semester.

The four weekend workshops were held during different seasons between the fall of 1988 and the summer of 1990. For each workshop session, participants met at the site on Saturday and Sunday for six hours per day and in the archaeology laboratory at PAL on two weeknights for orientation and cleaning of artifacts they had previously recovered (Figure 2.2). Weekend workshops were intended primarily for individuals who either were unable to attend the weekday field schools or who desired additional experience after completing a field school session. Family members and friends often enrolled together in the workshops. In order to reach a greater number of young students and teachers, seven school groups from across Rhode Island each conducted limited field and laboratory work as an additional aspect of the Lambert Farm program (Figure 2.3).

In addition to the field schools, weekend workshops, and school groups, there were two occasions (designated Phases One and Two) in which professional archaeologists from PAL joined members of the general public in the excavation of the site. These two phases were necessitated by a combination of surprising discoveries that had to be removed quickly. Aside from the 1980 testing by Morenon (1981), 18 separate phases of excavation, accounting for about 130 days, were completed prior to the site's destruction (Table 2.1). The more than 200 people who were trained in archaeological techniques at Lambert Farm constituted an eclectic group with an

FIGURE 2.2   Workshop participants excavating sample units along eastern boundary of Lambert Farm.

FIGURE 2.3   Students in junior high school workshop excavating sample units within southeastern portion of Lambert Farm under supervision of PAL archaeologist Robert Goodby (foreground) and volunteer John Damon.

TABLE 2.1
COMPLETED PHASES AND DATES OF ARCHAEOLOGICAL FIELDWORK
AT LAMBERT FARM

Phase	Dates
1988 Field School I (FS I 1988)[1]	June 13–July 1, 1988[2]
Phase One (1)	July 12–25 and 16 and 23, 1988
1988 Field School II (FS II 1988)	August 8–September 2, 1988
Brown University Anthropology 160 Class (BFM)	September 20–November 3, 1988[3]
Western Hills Jr. High School Workshop (WEST)	October 9 and 15, 1988
Winman Jr. High School Workshop (WIN)	October 17 and 24, 1988
1988 Fall Workshop (WS FALL 88)	October 29 and 30, 1988
Wheeler School Workshop (WLWS)	November 12 and 19, 1988
Guiteras School Workshop (GUIT)	May 15, 1989
1989 Spring Workshop (WS SPRING 89)	May 20 and 21, 1989
1989 Field School I (FS I 1989)	June 5–23, 1989
Phase Two (2)	July 15 and 16, 1989
1989 Field School II (FS II 1989)	July 31–August 25, 1989
Slater Jr. High School Workshop (SLAT)	May 31, 1990
Colt School Workshop (COLT)	June 1, 1990
Brown University Learning Community Workshop (BLC)	June 28, 1990
1990 Summer Workshop (WS SUMMER 90)	July 14, 15, 28, and 29, 1990
1990 Field School III[4] (FS III 1990)	July 30–August 24, 1990

[1] Abbreviation for cataloguing purposes.
[2] Unless otherwise specified, ranges of dates include only Monday through Friday.
[3] This Field Methods in Archaeology class met on Tuesday and Thursday afternoons.
[4] Sessions I and II of the 1990 field school were not offered due to insufficient enrollment.

enormous amount of energy, despite often working under strenuous conditions. They came from all walks of life—from third graders to senior citizens; from fishermen to homemakers. They also shared in the satisfaction of unearthing important Native American remains that otherwise would have been destroyed by construction.

SAMPLING STRATEGY

Once the goals and schedules were established, the next order of business was to decide on a strategy to sample the site. Sampling is a required and vital part of most archaeological projects due to budgetary and other constraints. Because it is often too expensive to excavate an entire site, archaeologists tend to focus on a portion or a sample of a site to investigate. The size of the sample is usually dictated by practical considerations, namely the availability of funding, time, and personnel. There is another reason for the importance of sampling in archaeology, particularly in the United States today. Since the 1970s, archaeological sites have come to be seen as limited, nonrenewable, and endangered resources. This view has led to a widespread movement, partly supported by legislation, among most American archaeologists to conserve sites. Conservation in archaeology essentially means that only significant sites that cannot be protected from destructive activities (i.e., development, erosion, etc.) should be fully excavated. This conservation ethic, as it is called, is based on the fact that the process of archaeological excavation destroys a site as a three-dimensional entity, though artifacts and information from the site may be recovered and preserved. The conservation ethic further dictates that nonthreatened sites should be left alone or at most tested with small samples so that they will remain a part of our heritage for the benefit of future generations and for future archaeologists who may have new questions and advanced technology with which to examine these sites in the years to come.

Many different ways exist to sample a site, but all may be separated into either random or systematic sampling. Choosing the type of sampling depends on project goals, as well as funding, personnel, and time limitations. Some projects use both sampling techniques at the same site. Random sampling, also called probabilistic sampling, attempts to generalize about an entire site, known as the population, based on a recovered sample. The locations of sample units, often holes dug at the site, are selected in random fashion so that bias is eliminated, and each unit has an equal chance of being chosen for testing. Once the locations of a sufficient number of sample units have been selected, statistical equations are applied to determine the probability that the remains recovered in the sample units are representative of the entire site. This is the same procedure used by pollsters in randomly selecting a sample of potential voters to predict the outcome of an election. Obviously, at an archaeological site the more units tested the greater the probability that the sample is representative of the whole site. But the only way one can be certain that the results are representative of the population is to excavate the entire site and obtain a 100% sample, which defeats the purpose of sampling in the first place. Instead, most archaeologists who use random sampling try to obtain a sample size large enough to reach at least 90% probability that the results are representative of the whole site.

Systematic sampling involves placing the sample units in a consistent fashion across the entire site or just within portions of a site that may contain more remains than in other parts of the site. In either case the sample units are located in a non-random, and thus biased, manner since the objective of systematic sampling is not necessarily to generalize about an entire site but to maximize the recovery of important remains. Often the sample units may be situated at the same interval along straight lines called transects. The location and direction of these transects are systematically selected in this example, though they would be randomly selected when using probabilistic sampling. This type of systematic sampling might be done as a preliminary step to identify patterns in the distribution of cultural materials at a site. Areas containing clusters of artifacts or shell deposits could then be systematically sampled more intensively with larger units. Sample units, whether for systematic or random sampling, may be of various shapes and sizes. Often they are square holes ranging from 50 cm to 2 m (about 1.6 to 6.5 ft) on a side.

In the Northeast, the vast majority of Native American archaeological sites are buried, some as deep as 8 feet. Unlike many other parts of the world, where sites are easily seen on the surface in the form of artifact scatters or high above the ground in the form of massive buildings detected by satellites, northeastern prehistoric sites are virtually invisible. They are primarily below ground because the raw materials used by Native Americans to make their structures were generally organic and thus eventually decomposed. Further, sedimentation and vegetation usually combine to cover the remains that did not perish.

Archaeology in the Northeast, by definition, means excavation. One must dig to find these hidden sites and to recover their contents (though ground-penetrating radar has been used with mixed success in locating some sites). But subsurface testing is long, back-breaking work that is often tedious. Why would anyone want to do it or, worse, pay to do it? Just ask anyone who has participated in a dig. The thrill of discovering an artifact that was last touched by human hands hundreds or thousands of years ago forges an immediate, personal connection to the past. It is a profound feeling that both the novice and seasoned excavator never forget and hope to experience anew with each shovel of dirt.

Well before fieldwork began at Lambert Farm, we needed to choose a sampling strategy. Despite our best intentions to dig the entire 1.8 acres on which six houses and a road were to be built, there was no escaping our funding, time, and personnel constraints. We were forced to accept the inevitable fact that we could not remove all the artifacts from the site. Indeed, most would be destroyed by the housing development as we could only recover a small sample. The question remained; which sampling technique would be the best? Probabilistic testing was ruled out, since it did not ensure even coverage of the site due to its random selection of sample unit locations. Since the site was to be obliterated by construction, we did not want to be forced to waste precious time and resources digging a lot of sample units randomly placed in areas where few or no artifacts might exist. Instead, we wanted some control and flexibility over the location of our sample units, and so we decided to use a two-staged approach.

The first stage involved systematic sampling of relatively small units situated along parallel transects distributed across the site. The second stage involved systematic placement of larger sample units in areas that we selected (nonrandomly). In this way, the initial results of the systematic sampling could be used to identify concentrations of artifacts and other remains, namely features, if they existed, within the entire 1.8 acres. A feature is a type of archaeological data that is nonportable, meaning it cannot be removed from a site intact. Instead, the parts of a feature are excavated individually. Examples include a burial, shell midden, and activity area, such as a place where stone tools were created or where food was cooked and eaten. Once located in the small test units, these important artifact clusters and features would then receive more intensive sampling, thus maximizing data recovery while minimizing our effort. In short, this strategy was consistent with our goal to obtain as much information as possible under the limiting conditions that beset the project.

Once on the site, we were faced with making several key decisions. The first was to decide where to place the datum, a fixed reference point at the site from which all the subsequent sample units would be located. The datum was arbitrarily placed along the southern boundary of the site in the middle of a proposed roadway (Spinnaker Lane), which was a hay field at the time (see Figure 1.3). A transit was used to measure the distance and angle from the datum to a permanent marker near the site—a telephone pole along Cowesett Road. Since this landmark remained in its exact location for the duration of our fieldwork, we could use it to make sure the location of the sample units was accurate.

Our next task was to set up the systematic sampling design, specifically, the arrangement of the transects and their associated subsurface sample units. Consistent with the standard size and shape of sample units placed along transects in much of the Northeast, we used 50 × 50-cm square holes, commonly referred to as shovel test pits (STPs). The heading of the transects then had to be determined. We chose an alignment of 10° magnetic north, since this was the direction of the soon-to-be constructed Spinnaker Lane, which was planned to run through the center of the housing development. The locations of all transects and STPs could then be easily transferred from our site map to the builder's plans.

We also needed to decide both the interval between transects, which would dictate the total number of transects, and the interval between STPs along each transect. We chose to place each transect at an interval of 2.5 m (8.2 ft), corresponding to a total of 40 transects. The same interval was selected for STP placement along each transect. More precisely, we placed the northeast corner of every STP along each transect at an interval of 2.5 m; occasionally, an obstruction, such as a rock or fence post, prevented the placement of the northeast corner of the STP at that spot, in which case the unit was moved slightly. In addition, the STP locations were offset by 1.25 m (4.1 ft) along alternating transects, while still maintaining the 2.5-m interval between STPs along each transect. This arrangement produced a pattern called a staggered grid, as opposed to a square grid which would have existed without the offset (Figure 2.4). A staggered grid was used because it is more effective and efficient in locating the same-size features than a square grid (Krakker et al. 1983; Whalen 1985). In light of existing time and funding limitations, the 2.5-meter interval represented the optimum distance to sample intensively the 1.8 acres with 100% statistical certainty of locating features, such as large shell middens and burials, 2.79 m (9.15 ft) or greater in diameter (Krakker et al. 1983). A longer interval would have resulted in the use of fewer STPs and thus less time and funding but a correspondingly lower probability of locating features. On the other hand, a shorter interval would have resulted in a higher likelihood of finding smaller features at the cost of completing more STPs and thus more time and funding. In sum, we could not have excavated as many STPs as we did with an interval less than 2.5 m, nor could we have found as many features as we did with an STP interval greater than 2.5 m.

When fieldwork began at Lambert Farm on June 13, 1988, the first area we sampled was the middle of the site. This area was selected at the outset because the developers wanted to construct Spinnaker Lane there that summer. This would allow machinery to gain access to the north end of the development, off the archaeological site, where land had to be cleared for house construction. We chose the centerline of proposed Spinnaker Lane as our first transect, labelled T01 (see Figure 1.3). At the southernmost point on this transect was the previously established site datum, which also served as the northeastern corner of our first STP, designated T01-0. This area, however, had been disturbed by topsoil removal some years before our project. Since we were reluctant to waste time and effort within areas that had little likelihood of containing archaeological material, we placed the second STP 10 m down the transect at T01-10, skipping over the intervening locations of STPs at 2.5-m intervals. During this first field school session, we also completed other STPs at 10-m intervals along T01 and adjacent transects. Over the next two years, most of the

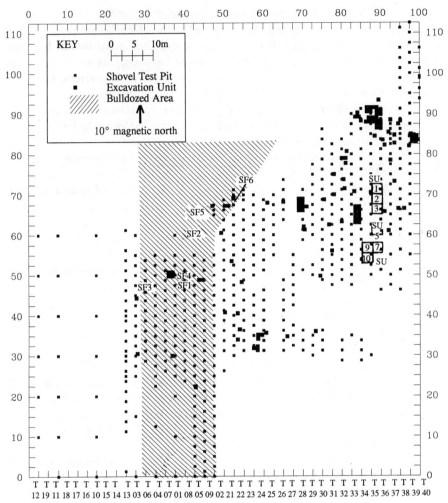

FIGURE 2.4   Testing strategy at Lambert Farm, showing locations of completed sample units, shell deposits (SF), plow-zone-stripped units (SU), and area bulldozed for Spinnaker Lane construction.

remaining STPs at Lambert Farm would be dug at the 2.5-m interval, as originally planned. Those STPs that were not completed were located primarily in the western portion of the site, an area in which we discovered relatively few artifacts and thus sampled less intensively (Figure 2.4).

EXCAVATION PROCEDURES

Each STP was excavated in the same manner. First, the 50×50-cm unit was measured along the transect, and four metal spikes were inserted at the corners of the square. Working in crews of two, the excavator began by using a spade shovel to cut into the sod along the sides of the STP, connecting the four spikes. The sod from the hay field was carefully removed in pieces and placed in the partner's two-legged sifting screen, which consisted of 0.25-in wire mesh. The reason for sifting the sod at Lambert Farm, as well as at most sites in the Northeast, is because the site had been plowed during at least the past century. Plowing of a site tends to lift artifacts from lower levels in the ground closer to the surface, within a deposit referred to as the plow zone; experienced collectors of prehistoric artifacts, so-called avocational archaeologists, often focus their search in fields just after they have been plowed so remains can be easily spotted on the surface. Indeed, many of the participants at Lambert Farm were astonished to find ancient Native American artifacts in the sod, mixed in with the debris of our own culture, such as glass, nails, and soda cans.

Throughout the excavation of the hole, the digger made sure to keep the sidewalls straight in order to identify the different layers of the soil, also called stratigraphy, which were precisely recorded on the completion of the STP. Maintaining straight sidewalls was also vital for making accurate measurements of the levels in the STP. We dug most STPs in 10-cm (about 4-in) levels; occasionally 5-cm levels were used for finer control when especially important remains were encountered. Excavating in levels was done to separate artifacts recovered at different depths, since the depth at which an artifact is found may provide an estimate of how old it is. Based on a principle borrowed from geology, namely the Law of Superposition, the deeper an object is buried the older its age. At an archaeological site that has been plowed, however, this principle does not hold for remains displaced within the plow zone.

Within the first 10 cm below ground surface, the excavator placed soil, a few shovelfuls at a time, in the sifting screen. With a few vigorous shakes, soil less than 0.25 inch in diameter passed through the mesh, leaving behind larger items, such as rocks and often cultural material. All archaeological remains found in the screen were placed in a plastic zip-lock bag with a tag indicating the appropriate context— the site, unit number, transect, and depth—along with other important information, such as the names of the crew and the date. This procedure of identifying and recovering artifacts in the screen usually created much commotion. Shouts of excitement were intermittently heard across the site on the recovery of Native American tools, especially projectile points and pottery sherds, prompting people to run from all directions to see what was found. Picking out other prehistoric remains, particularly chipping debris, in the screen at first required considerable time and effort for the inexperienced crew, but after only a few hours of training their eyes to know what to look for, it became quite easy. Nevertheless, it seemed that participants were constantly asking, "Is this something?" A negative response from the field assistants or me resulted in immediate disappointment. But more often than not, I conservatively replied, "Keep it just in case."

Once the screen was scanned, a trained field assistant or I was called over to give it one last look before the items were dumped out. The excavator then added more soil from the square hole to the screen, and this process continued until the bottom of the level was reached at 10 cm below ground surface. The excavator double-checked the depth after using a trowel to level the floor of the hole and straighten the sidewalls. Any features, such as shell deposits and hearths, were mapped for each level in which they appeared and were noted on standardized forms, along with an inventory of recovered materials by level and any other important observations.

Each participant also kept a field journal to record similar information. This turned out to be especially helpful in correcting inconsistencies such as mislabelling provenience tags. Human error is an unavoidable part of any fieldwork operation, and great pains were taken at Lambert Farm to minimize it as much as possible.

After the last screenful of dirt from the level was sifted, soil from the next level (10–20 cm [about 4–8 in] below ground surface) was added to the screen in the manner just described, and all recovered artifacts were put in their own bag for the level. Excavation continued this way, one 10-cm level at a time, until glacial subsoil was reached, usually around 50 cm deep. The glacial deposit, often consisting of gravel, was culturally sterile because it was laid down over 10,000 years ago when the glacier was melting, well before any prehistoric residents lived at Lambert Farm. On a few occasions, we came across archaeological remains more than 50 cm below ground; they were deposited in holes originally dug into the glacial subsoil by the Native Americans and were later filled in. When the bottom of an STP was reached, a profile of one of its walls was drawn to record the soil layers and any anomalies. The stratigraphy usually consisted of three layers: the sod and soil at the top, termed the humus; the thick, dark brown sand and silt in the middle that contained the majority of the plow zone and recovered artifacts; and the light brown sand and gravel of the glacial deposit at the bottom. It normally took a crew of two people about two hours to complete excavating, sifting, and recording at one STP.

During all field school and workshop sessions, larger holes, called excavation units (EUs), were also dug. The EUs consisted of varying shapes and sizes, mostly 1 × 1-m (about 3.3 × 3.3-ft) squares, and were systematically placed next to numerous STPs containing features and important artifacts, especially projectile points and prehistoric pottery sherds (see Figure 2.4). These larger units were part of the second stage of our sampling strategy. Regardless of their shape and size, all EUs were excavated in the same way as the STPs, using either 5-cm or 10-cm levels depending on the contents of the unit. In addition to a spade shovel to slice the ground along the sides of the EU, we used a flat-bottom shovel and a trowel to carefully peel away the layers of the soil. A considerable amount of prehistoric material was often recovered in each EU, not just because the hole was larger than STPs (most were at least four times as large), but also because the EUs were intentionally placed where a lot of remains were already found in the STPs. As a result, a crew of three or four people with two or three sifting screens usually worked a full day to finish an EU. If a dense feature, such as a thick shell deposit, was encountered, however, excavation of the EU crawled at a snail's pace, sometimes taking up to four days to complete.

Excavating a feature was done in 5-cm levels and required more steps. Most important, the feature's surrounding soil, called the matrix, had to be removed before the feature itself within each 5-cm level. Any archaeological remains found in the matrix were placed in a bag, separate from materials recovered in the feature at the same level. Thus, the crew needed to work in an especially well-organized, coordinated, and precise manner when dealing with a feature. Once removed, there was no second chance to dig the feature again. At the bottom of the level, both the feature and the matrix were drawn and photographed. We even used soil color charts, resembling paint chips, to record the exact color of the deposits. The next 5-cm level was then excavated and so on until the feature was no longer visible. At this point, digging returned to 10-cm levels until sterile glacial subsoil was reached. The work at the EU finally came to a halt after the stratigraphy of the pit's walls was drawn and photographed, especially the walls that still contained remnants of the feature in their profile.

Some of the more challenging and exciting EUs in which we worked were those that contained multiple features beginning and ending at different levels and eventually spreading to adjacent EUs. Such features were usually dense shell deposits, each containing an abundance of material that we placed in dozens of plastic bags, in addition to often thousands of shells that we did not retain. We could not possibly keep all the shells from every feature, nor could we take column samples from selected shell features, due to the exorbitant costs needed to clean, catalogue, analyze, and store the thousands of shells. Column samples are typically excavated from sidewalls of completed units, partly to analyze the stratigraphy of the deposit. At shell-bearing sites, in particular, taking column samples may be helpful, especially when archaeologists attempt to estimate the contribution of shellfish to the overall diet of the sites' inhabitants (e.g., Glasgow 1996). At Lambert Farm, however, such an estimate could not be made accurately since obtaining a representative sample of shellfish remains was not possible, given the project's time and funding limitations. Consequently, we considered the shells that we excavated as mostly redundant information, so collecting a few was almost as good as collecting all. That is why we removed only a small sample of every shellfish species observed in each 5-cm level of a feature. We still recorded the names of every species we saw and their approximate densities (i.e., light, medium, heavy) by feature level. The exception to this rule was the collection of all complete shells of the species *Mercenaria mercenaria,* commonly called quahog, from excavated features. These shells were especially important for later analysis, as were soil and radiocarbon samples taken from several features. The subsequent testing of these samples is discussed in the next chapter.

In retrospect, properly excavating a multicomponent site as large and complex as Lambert Farm was a real challenge. The method we used, shovel test pits and excavation units systematically placed on a grid system spaced over several field seasons, was selected out of necessity due to the project's various constraints. While we were successful in recovering copious amounts of archaeological materials and some rather unusual features, our sampling strategy and the use of mainly arbitrary stratigraphy made it difficult to gain a good understanding of the remains' horizontal relationships across the site. As elaborated in the next chapter, the use of widely separated sample units prevented us from cleaning off even one living surface (though disturbances to Lambert Farm caused by plowing made it exceedingly unlikely that any living surfaces would have been preserved). This problem also applied to the excavation of several dense shell features at the site. Even if we took column samples from these features and had all the time and money in the world, we still would have been unable to delineate fully the complex stratigraphy of Lambert Farm's shell deposits, given their coarse nature and their often multiple episodes of use. If we had the chance to excavate Lambert Farm and its shell features again under the same circumstances, would we have done it any differently? I suspect, for the most part, probably not, since no sampling strategy could solve the problems we encountered in understanding horizontal relationships across the site, as well as within individual dense shell deposits.

PHASES ONE AND TWO AND UNUSUAL SAMPLE UNITS

The participants in 16 of the 18 phases of fieldwork at Lambert Farm performed all the techniques described so far, under professional supervision. Phases One and Two involved the combined work of PAL archaeologists and former field school and workshop participants. Phase One occurred at the end of the first session of the 1988 field school after a highly unusual prehistoric deposit, designated Feature 2, was discovered within STP T01-50 and adjacent EU 3, both in the middle of the proposed Spinnaker Lane (Figure 2.4). At this point, we knew that part of the feature contained the remains of a dog interred beneath an extremely thick accumulation of buried shells and other objects, as discussed in detail in Chapter 4. We did not know what else was in the feature, since there was no time left in the session to continue working. The problem was that construction of Spinnaker Lane would destroy the unexcavated portion of the feature before the start of the second session later that summer. We were faced with a crisis, and we had not even finished the first field school! Once again Alan Leveillee and I, as the project's codirectors, together with Paul Robinson, approached the developers. This time we met at the site on a hot afternoon in June to show off what remained of the feature and to discuss a plan for its removal, knowing full well that the developers were not legally required to respond to our wishes. The meeting went better than we imagined. Sensitive to the significance of what we had partly unearthed, the developers voluntarily agreed to continue to delay construction of Spinnaker Lane for two more weeks. Needless to say, we were overjoyed, but two weeks gave us very little breathing room to accomplish our task.

With the miraculous assistance of Paul Robinson, PAL received an emergency grant from the Rhode Island Historical Preservation Commission to excavate the remaining portion of the feature and to determine whether similar features also lay within the road construction area. During our two-week abbreviated miniproject (July 12–25, 1988), PAL staff archaeologists, including myself, worked furiously to remove what was left of Feature 2. We also worked hard at fending off numerous television and newspaper reporters, as well as other curious observers, who invaded the site for a peek at the flurry of activity surrounding the feature. An additional component of Phase One included PAL archaeologists and their families, as well as former field school participants, all of whom volunteered to dig STPs and EUs in oppressive heat on two successive Saturdays during the road construction delay. My fiancée and I worked together at the site on the second Saturday, a rare occurrence for us and even more remarkable considering our wedding was one week away! In any event, Phase One was a huge success and an extremely rewarding experience for all who helped.

A nearly identical situation occurred during the first session of the 1989 field school, almost one year to the day from the discovery of Feature 2. A strikingly similar prehistoric deposit, designated Feature 22, was encountered within STP T35-90 and adjacent EU 55 (Figure 2.4). Like Feature 2, this deposit contained the grave of a dog below a dense accumulation of buried shells and other debris, also described in Chapter 4. The problem here was twofold. We could not completely excavate the feature before the end of the first session of the 1989 field school, and the second field school session was scheduled to start in 5 weeks from when we discovered Feature 22. So we decided to stop excavating the feature and immediately covered it with soil to keep it concealed until a second phase, Phase Two, could be pulled together. Within a few weeks, a group of volunteers from PAL staff and former field school and workshop sessions was organized, as no funding was available this time to excavate the feature. Fieldwork was performed on both days of a sultry July weekend, between the end of the first session and the beginning of the second session of the 1989 field school. It was quite a hectic two days. Besides the excavation, we had a film crew on site documenting the dig as part of our *Back to the Past* videotape. Despite the fast-paced work, we were unable to remove all of Feature 22 over the weekend. The rest of the feature was later excavated by Alan and me during the second session of the 1989 field school.

Not all units completed at Lambert Farm were excavated as STPs and EUs. During the second session of the 1988 field school, while construction of Spinnaker Lane was occurring, we closely watched the bulldozer's blade dig into the ground to see if unknown shell features were encountered; this kind of feature is much more easily spotted than others because of its thick accumulation of shells. Indeed, not surprisingly, six previously unidentified shell deposits, designated SF1–6, were discovered by the bulldozer, which had removed only the top portion of these dense features (Figure 2.4). After asking a cooperative bulldozer operator to stop for a few minutes, we quickly mapped, photographed, and excavated what remained of these six deposits (Figure 1.5, page 12). The archaeological material from each feature was removed in one level since the ground surface had just been obliterated.

Other units were also sampled in a manner different from that used to dig the STPs and EUs. This occurred toward the end of the last field session of 1990, the final period of fieldwork before the site was to be destroyed by house construction. We asked the developers for one last favor—the use of the bulldozer for a morning. As usual, they graciously agreed but wondered, understandably so, why we would need such a machine. While usually a destroyer of sites, the bulldozer can play a useful role in archaeological excavation, even at sites containing fragile remains, such as Lambert Farm. We selected for further investigation a 5 × 20-m (about 16 × 65-ft) area situated between transects T34 and T36 in the eastern portion of the site. This was where we had found unusually rich deposits in several STPs and EUs, leading us to suspect the presence of features, possibly even burials. We lacked the time to excavate by shovel the numerous EUs needed to verify our hunch. But now we had the use of a powerful machine that could dig for us. At our direction, the bulldozer carefully removed the plow-zone deposit, roughly the top 25–30 cm (about 10–12 in) of soil, from the 100-m^2 (about 1075-ft^2) area. After this was done, amazingly in less than 30 minutes, we plotted seven 2.5 × 2.5-m units, designated SU1–3,5,7,9,10, within this stripped area (Figure 2.4). Using shovels, we then quickly scraped off about 15–20 cm (about 6–8 in) of soil from these large units (Figure 2.5). In short, we performed this exercise within a potentially sensitive area

FIGURE 2.5   Field school participants completing plow-zone-stripped units (foreground) in the area designated SU1-3, 5, 7, 9, 10.

as a last-minute attempt to identify any features that might have been buried beneath the plow zone and subsequently exposed by quick topsoil removal. With mixed emotions of disappointment and relief, we discovered only one feature, a small shell deposit, and found no burials.

A few days later, on August 24, 1990, fieldwork stopped for the last time at Lambert Farm. The hay field and overgrown animal corrals where the site was located when the dig began in 1988 now looked like a mine field. There were holes strewn everywhere, intentionally left open so that the time that might have been used to backfill them was instead spent digging new ones. The holes reminded us how much we had accomplished over the past 2 years. In all, a total of 523 STPs and 122 EUs were completed by more than 200 people, spanning some 130 days and 18 phases of fieldwork at Lambert Farm. This amounted to more than 4,400 cubic feet (about 125 cubic meters) of earth that was dug by shovel but accounted for a sample fraction of only 3.68% of the testable area within the National Register portion of the site. Put another way, more than 95% of the site's 1.8 acres was not investigated at all. Nevertheless, on the basis of the total volume of unearthed soil, Lambert Farm remains one of the most thoroughly hand-excavated sites in the Northeast. It also contained an enormous amount of archaeological remains. We turn to the next chapter to examine the site's assemblage and to discuss its laboratory processing, analysis, and interpretations.

CHAPTER 3

Laboratory Processing, Analysis, and Interpretations

With the completion of fieldwork at Lambert Farm on August 24, 1990, a major part of the investigation was accomplished. But the end of the excavation, as exhausting as it was, did not bring an end to the research. Actually, the dig was only one step. As part of our research design, we needed to interpret and explain what we had brought back from the site so that the results could be written and published. What did it all mean? Before we could begin to answer such a broad question, as well as many other specific ones framed in this chapter, we still had a considerable amount of work to finish. We first needed to process the more than 56,000 archaeological specimens collected from the site and then analyze many of them. Much of this material, both the expected and unexpected, is discussed in this chapter and the next. But the site's most significant and certainly most exciting discoveries, the dog burials, receive detailed treatment in Chapter 4.

LABORATORY PROCESSING

It is often said that for every day spent excavating in the field at least five days are spent processing and analyzing in the lab. This statement certainly applied to the Lambert Farm project as research continued for four straight years after the fieldwork had stopped, and additional research of the collection is still planned. During each phase of testing at Lambert Farm, all recovered cultural materials were returned to the laboratory at PAL for simultaneous or subsequent processing; the one exception was the BFM Phase in which much of the processing was performed in the archaeology laboratory at Brown University by the students in the Field Methods class during the 1988 fall semester (Figure 3.1). This way each participant in the fieldwork also contributed to the laboratory work, which was a tremendous help in light of the enormous size of the assemblage. Also, the laboratory processing provided an opportunity for each person to see what others in the same phase had found at the site. Often, unusual items that were considered ordinary or simply overlooked when they were excavated in the field were "discovered" in the lab during processing.

Five steps were performed in the laboratory processing: cleaning, drying, sorting, rebagging, and cataloguing. Every object, except charcoal, was cleaned by either dry- or wet-brushing in order to facilitate identification and for accurate recording during cataloguing. Prehistoric pottery sherds, metallic artifacts, and organic materials were gently cleaned with a dry, soft-bristle toothbrush. Other remains, such as

FIGURE 3.1   Brown University students cataloguing Lambert Farm artifacts.

stone tools, chipping debris, and historic ceramics, were immersed in water and washed with a soft-bristle toothbrush. Immediately following cleaning, the items were placed on paper towels to air dry. We made sure that the provenience tags were removed from their bags and put next to the associated objects. Once dry, the clean specimens were sorted into groups of noncultural and cultural remains. Only cultural materials were retained and placed in new plastic bags, each containing the appropriate provenience tag. Participants in all but a few of the phases were able to clean, sort, dry, and rebag all the archaeological remains that they had previously recovered in their respective phases. Those items that were not processed in this way were done so later by students under my supervision at Colgate University, where I had begun teaching in 1989.

After all of the above procedures were completed, we were ready to perform the last step in the laboratory processing—cataloguing the cultural materials. Cataloguing was done in two ways: direct computer input and hand recording and subsequent computer input. In both situations, all prehistoric tools were drawn on individual artifact cards, which also contained relevant provenience and attribute information (i.e., size, style, color, weight, and so on). Direct computer input was then performed by each participant under supervision of lab assistants. The procedure involved entering provenience and attribute information for every object, not just the tools, into a computer software catalogue program, created by PAL, known as ADAM2. Given the enormity of the assemblage, however, it could not be entirely catalogued in this manner by the participants of each phase. Many of the remaining materials were catalogued using computers by two grant-supported research assistants at PAL, who worked for a total of 560 hours over a 10-month period in 1988 and 1989. The second method of cataloguing involved first recording all provenience and attribute data by hand on a form and then entering this information into the ADAM2 computer catalogue program. By maintaining a separate handwritten form, the same or different group of cataloguers could enter data into the computer at a later, more convenient time. Also, the handwritten form provided a way to check for errors in subsequent computer files and was a backup in the event that the computerized data were lost or accidentally erased. During the 27 months of excavation, hand cataloguing was only performed in the BFM phase. But because of the large number of remains recovered by the Brown University students, they were unable to complete the subsequent computer catalogue before the end of the semester.

All recovered materials that had not been catalogued when fieldwork ceased in 1990 were transported to Colgate University. There they were catalogued by hand and computerized by me and student volunteers and work-study assistants under my supervision. We finally completed the cataloguing and the computer recording in February 1993. Thus, all the cultural remains excavated at Lambert Farm, more than 56,000 specimens, were eventually cleaned, sorted, catalogued, bagged, and boxed, bringing to a close the lengthy task of laboratory processing. They are now curated at the Rhode Island Historical Preservation Commission.

Various kinds of analyses were performed on many of the Lambert Farm materials. Some of the remains were analyzed at the time laboratory processing was still ongoing, while others were analyzed several months later. In most cases, specialists conducted the analyses, which is typical of archaeological projects due to the interdisciplinary nature of the research. The remainder of this chapter discusses the analyses and subsequent interpretations of the Lambert Farm assemblage, excluding the three dog burials.

AGE OF THE SITE

One of the basic questions asked about any site is "How old is it?" The answer is usually determined, at least in part, by radiocarbon dating, which calculates the age of organic material based on the amount of the isotope carbon 14 that has not yet decayed in the object. Since funding was limited, we had to choose our radiocarbon samples wisely, despite an abundance of organic remains. A total of 10 samples were taken from features below the plow zone at Lambert Farm. We intentionally did not select samples from the plow zone since they had been displaced from their original contexts. On the other hand, dating organic material in an undisturbed feature would help us understand the age of the feature's other associated items. Nine samples consisting of quahog shells, each sample weighing about 50 gm (about 1.1 lbs), were submitted to Beta Analytic, Inc., a radiocarbon dating laboratory in Miami, Florida. The other sample, weighing 2.3 gm, consisted of three rib fragments from the dog buried in Feature 22. This sample was processed by the accelerator mass spectrometry (AMS) technique at the NSF-Arizona AMS Facility at the University of Arizona in Tucson. The AMS technique requires a much smaller sample than conventional radiocarbon dating and was thus chosen in order to minimize the destruction of the skeletal remains.

All radiocarbon dates are statistical approximations of actual ages and as such are not 100% accurate. When the results of radiocarbon dating come back from the lab in about 30 days, except for AMS samples which take up to four months, they

TABLE 3.1
RADIOCARBON SAMPLES AND DATES FROM LAMBERT FARM

Lab Number	Provenience	Material Weight	C-14 Age ± 1 s.d. (uncorrected[1])	C-14 Age ± 2 s.d. (calibrated[2])
Beta-27937	EU 3, Fea. 2, 70–80 cm	Shell 50.0 gm	870 ± 80 B.P.[3] A.D. 1000–1160	1140–660 B.P. A.D. 810–1290
Beta-27938	EU 5, Fea. 4, 30–40 cm	Shell 52.7 gm	900 ± 70 B.P. A.D. 980–1120	1150–690 B.P. A.D. 800–1260
Beta-52440	EU 13, 40–50 cm	Shell 52.5 gm	930 ± 60 B.P. A.D. 960–1080	1170–730 B.P. A.D. 780–1220
Beta-27936	EU 18, 30–40 cm	Shell 54.3 gm	720 ± 60 B.P. A.D. 1170–1290	940–560 B.P. A.D. 1010–1390
Beta-27939	EU 23, 20–30 cm	Shell 52.7 gm	1060 ± 60 B.P. A.D. 830–950	1280–900 B.P. A.D. 670–1050
Beta-28499	EU 38, Fea. 15, 40–50 cm	Shell 51.9 gm	610 ± 70 B.P. A.D. 1270–1410	870–490 B.P. A.D. 1080–1460
Beta-43486	EU 55, Fea. 22, 80–90 cm	Shell 55.4 gm	610 ± 70 B.P. A.D. 1270–1410	870–490 B.P. A.D. 1080–1460
AA-11784	EU 62, Fea. 22, 80–90 cm	Bone 2.3 gm	810 ± 45 B.P. A.D. 1095–1185	790–660 B.P. A.D. 1160–1290
Beta-52441	T08-38.75, Fea. 5, 30–40 cm	Shell 53.0 gm	880 ± 60 B.P. A.D. 1010–1130	1120–680 B.P. A.D. 830–1270
Beta-28339	T37-72.5, Fea. 12, 30–40 cm	Shell 52.2 gm	860 ± 90 B.P. A.D. 1000–1180	1140–650 B.P. A.D. 810–1300

[1] Dates reported by Beta Analytic and the NSF-Arizona AMS Facility represent a 66% confidence interval and are RCYBP (radiocarbon years before A.D. 1950). By international convention, the half-life of radiocarbon is taken as 5,568 years and 95% of the activity of the National Bureau of Standards of Oxalic Acid (original batch) used as the modern standard. The Beta Analytic dates are not corrected for DeVries effect, reservoir effect, or isotope fractionation in nature ($\delta^{13}C$). The AMS date is a conventional date and is corrected for $\delta^{13}C$ ($\delta^{13}C$ value is –14.0%) (Donahue 1994:1) but is not calibrated.

[2] Calibrated dates represent a 95% confidence interval. Reference for the calibration data set used for all shell samples is Stuiver and Braziunas (1993) and for the AMS sample is Stuiver and Pearson (1993). In addition, the following options were selected in calculating the calibrated dates of all shell samples: laboratory error multiplier (K) = 1 (Murry Tamers, personal communication 1993); $\delta^{13}C$ correction for isotope fractionation = 0 ± 2 (Stuiver and Reimer 1993b:Table 1); and reservoir correction (R) for marine samples = –85 ± 75 (Stuiver and Braziunas 1993:Figure 16). For the AMS sample: K = 1 (Donahue 1994:1).

[3] Years before present.

usually have been calculated at a single standard deviation. Put simply, this means that there is a 66% chance that the actual age of the sample falls within the range specified by the lab. This is why all radiocarbon dates are expressed with a plus or minus factor, which refers to the time range.

Table 3.1 lists information on the 10 radiocarbon samples from Lambert Farm. All of the Beta Analytic dates were uncorrected, which means that the effects of a variable amount of radiocarbon in the atmosphere and thus in all living organisms were not factored in the results. Radiocarbon dates can be corrected by using known, accurate dates from tree rings as a means for calibration. For the 10 Lambert Farm dates, I used the calibration computer program, CALIB REV 3.0.3 (Stuiver and Reimer 1993a, 1993b), created by the University of Washington Quaternary Iso tope Laboratory. Calibrating each of these 10 dates, even the AMS date which was corrected, resulted in a new date with two standard deviations, meaning that the actual age of each sample falls within the newly computed range at a 95% level of confidence. As was emphasized to me by the codirector of Beta Analytic, Murry Tamers (personal communication 1993), however, the results of calibration are based on a model not yet tested. Nevertheless, the following discussion of the ages of the radiocarbon samples from Lambert Farm is limited to the calibrated time ranges.

Eight of the 10 radiocarbon samples have different calibrated date ranges; even the two samples (EU 38 and EU 55) with identical ranges may not actually be the same age. Four calibrated date ranges (from samples EU 18, EU 38, EU 55, and EU 62) are limited to the Late Woodland period (ca. 1000–450 B.P. [years before present]), and the remaining six span both the Middle Woodland (ca. 1650–1000 B.P.) and Late Woodland periods. While it is possible that up to six samples date to the Middle Woodland period, it is striking that all 10 could date to the Late Woodland period, given their respective calibrated ranges.

Similarly, we cannot state with certainty whether these 10 calibrated date ranges represent 10 separate episodes of settlement at Lambert Farm. It is likely, however, that they indicate at least two occupations—one that occurred for an unknown duration between 790–730 B.P. and the other sometime between 1280–900 B.P. This is suggested by two observations in Table 3.1: (1) the absence of a single time span that is shared by all 10 calibrated ranges; and (2) the occurrence of a single time span (790–730 B.P.) that overlaps all calibrated ranges except one (1280–900 B.P. from sample EU 23). Unfortunately, because radiocarbon dates are statistical approximations and because they are expressed with a time range, I am unable to be more definitive in estimating an age for the site occupation(s).

In addition to the radiocarbon dates, the age of the prehistoric site may be estimated based on the presence of specific artifacts that are believed to represent various periods. These diagnostic artifacts, as they are termed, include certain styles or types of projectile points and ceramics. Much effort was made during the Lambert Farm fieldwork to locate these kinds of artifacts, especially in excavation units. Although they cannot be directly radiocarbon dated because of their inorganic raw material, the age of diagnostic artifacts is reconstructed from their frequent recovery in contexts that contain radiocarbon-dated materials from numerous sites in the Northeast. For instance, finding the projectile point type identified as Levanna at a site would enable me to date one occupation to the Late Woodland period, since this diagnostic artifact has been recovered in the region on several occasions in direct association with radiocarbon samples dating between 1000–450 B.P. After scores of these associations between radiocarbon dates and various styles of projectile points have been amassed, a typology can be developed, indicating which diagnostic types tend to represent which periods for a particular geographic area.

A total of 58 diagnostic projectile points were recovered from Lambert Farm, indicating the Late Archaic, Transitional Archaic, and Early, Middle, and Late Woodland periods, based on Ritchie's (1971) typology; some of these tools are illustrated in Figures 3.2 and 3.3. More than half (34 points, 58.6%) date to the Late Woodland period and consist of 31 Levanna and 3 Madison points. The other periods indicated, in descending order, are the Late Archaic (ca. 5000–3000 B.P.,

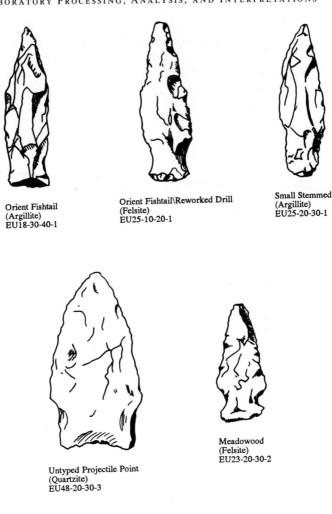

Orient Fishtail
(Argillite)
EU18-30-40-1

Orient Fishtail\Reworked Drill
(Felsite)
EU25-10-20-1

Small Stemmed
(Argillite)
EU25-20-30-1

Untyped Projectile Point
(Quartzite)
EU48-20-30-3

Meadowood
(Felsite)
EU23-20-30-2

cm

FIGURE 3.2   Illustration of selected projectile points recovered from Lambert Farm.

3000–1000 B.C.), 11 points, 19%, represented by 9 Small Stemmed and 2 Squib-nocket Triangle points; Transitional Archaic (ca. 3600–2500 B.P., 1600–500 B.C.), 10 points, 17.2%, represented by 6 Orient Fishtail, 2 Atlantic, and 2 Wayland Notched points; Middle Woodland, 2 points, 3.5%, represented by 1 Fox Creek and 1 Jack's Reef Corner-Notched point; and Early Woodland (ca. 3000–1600 B.P., 1000 B.C.–A.D. 350), 1 point, 1.7%, represented by 1 Meadowood point.

Analysis of many of the prehistoric pottery sherds recovered from Lambert Farm shows a similar pattern. Of the hundreds of prehistoric ceramic remains, the total weight of which exceeded 1,000 gm (2.2 lbs), 129 were examined by Goodby (1993) of the University of New Hampshire. Goodby selected only the best pre-

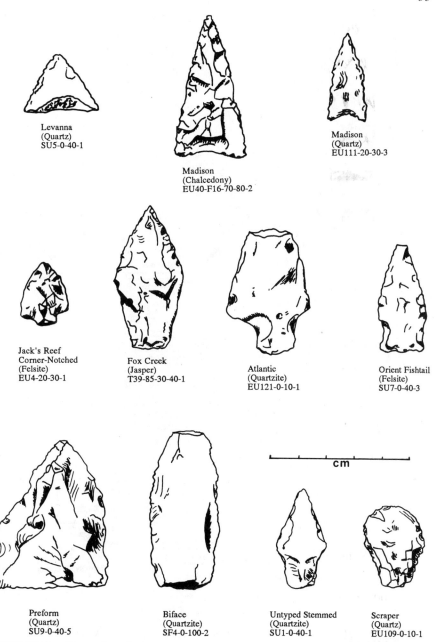

Levanna
(Quartz)
SU5-0-40-1

Madison
(Chalcedony)
EU40-F16-70-80-2

Madison
(Quartz)
EU111-20-30-3

Jack's Reef
Corner-Notched
(Felsite)
EU4-20-30-1

Fox Creek
(Jasper)
T39-85-30-40-1

Atlantic
(Quartzite)
EU121-0-10-1

Orient Fishtail
(Felsite)
SU7-0-40-3

cm

Preform
(Quartz)
SU9-0-40-5

Biface
(Quartzite)
SF4-0-100-2

Untyped Stemmed
(Quartzite)
SU1-0-40-1

Scraper
(Quartz)
EU109-0-10-1

FIGURE 3.3   Illustration of selected projectile points, preform, biface, and scraper recovered from Lambert Farm.

served specimens, specifically, rim and body sherds with intact and exterior surfaces; several of these sherds exhibit intricate designs (Figure 3.4). The results of his study indicate that most of these sherds possess traits characteristic of the Late Woodland period in southern New England, such as fine shell temper (tiny particles

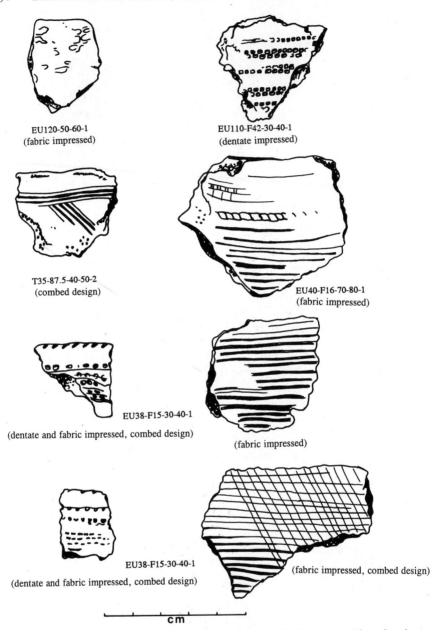

EU120-50-60-1
(fabric impressed)

EU110-F42-30-40-1
(dentate impressed)

T35-87.5-40-50-2
(combed design)

EU40-F16-70-80-1
(fabric impressed)

EU38-F15-30-40-1
(dentate and fabric impressed, combed design)

(fabric impressed)

EU38-F15-30-40-1
(dentate and fabric impressed, combed design)

(fabric impressed, combed design)

cm

FIGURE 3.4   Illustration of selected prehistoric ceramic sherds recovered from Lambert
Farm.

of crushed shell mixed with the clay for added cohesion), combed design, and fabric-
impressed exterior. Some of the remaining sherds contain coarse grit temper,
strongly reminiscent of Early Woodland Vinette I pottery in general (Goodby 1993),
while others contain grit temper that resembles both Middle and Late Woodland ceramics from the vicinity of Narragansett Bay (Goodby 1992). The sherds illustrated
in Figure 3.4 contain shell temper.

It is important to stress, however, that some presumably diagnostic projectile points and pottery sherds may not necessarily have been limited to a discrete time range but rather spanned more than one prehistoric period. For instance, it is likely that some, if not all, of the recovered Small Stemmed and Squibnocket Triangle points were used only during the Woodland period at Lambert Farm, in light of the abundant evidence for occupation of the site during this period. Both projectile point types have been recovered in Woodland period contexts from several sites elsewhere in southern New England (Bernstein 1993; Filios 1989; Hoffman 1983; Juli and McBride 1984; Kerber 1984). Thus, diagnostic artifacts are best used in conjunction with radiocarbon dates in estimating the age of a site. Dating a site based solely on diagnostic artifacts leaves much room for uncertainty.

Indeed, two discrepancies were noted in comparing the time periods, represented by recovered projectile point types, with the radiocarbon dates of stratigraphically associated shells from features. The only projectile points found in features in association with (i.e., the same depth as) radiocarbon-dated material (i.e., shell) are an Orient Fishtail and a Meadowood point. The Orient Fishtail point, presumably dating to the Transitional Archaic period (ca. 3600–2500 B.P., 1600–500 B.C.), was recovered associated with the radiocarbon sample from EU 18, which has a calibrated date range of 940–560 B.P. (i.e., Late Woodland period). The Meadowood point, presumably indicating the Early Woodland period (ca. 3000–1600 B.P., 1000 B.C.–A.D. 350), was found in association with the radiocarbon sample from EU 23, which has a calibrated date range of 1280–900 B.P. (i.e., Middle Woodland/Late Woodland periods). There are at least seven possible explanations for these discrepancies: (1) The projectile points are not diagnostic of the respective periods previously thought and thus were actually used during the later times represented by the respective associated radiocarbon dates; (2) the point types have not been accurately identified and were used during the times represented by the respective associated radiocarbon dates; (3) the radiocarbon dates are inaccurate (due to error, contamination, etc.), and thus the points were actually used during the earlier periods of which they are believed to be respectively diagnostic; (4) the points were used and discarded during their respective diagnostic periods but then later found and reused during the times represented by the respective associated radiocarbon dates; (5) the features in which both points were discovered were disturbed, and thus both points were not actually associated with the respective radiocarbon-dated shell at the same depth; (6) a combination of the above factors; and (7) unknown factors are at work.

In sum, while asking how old a site is seems like a straightforward question, the answer is often unclear. This is especially true for Lambert Farm, not only because of the limited resolution in the time ranges of both the radiocarbon dates and the diagnostic artifacts, but also because of the lack of stratigraphic evidence for dating the site. At some undisturbed sites buried by deep deposits, such as floodplain sediments, discrete living floors may be detected in the stratigraphy, indicating specific occupation layers and a relative chronology of settlement. This was not the case at Lambert Farm, however, where archaeological remains within 30 cm or so of the modern ground surface were disturbed by plowing over the past few hundred years. Even in features situated below the plow zone, such as pits and burials, the stratigraphy, admittedly, was too complex to discern separate living surfaces. Nevertheless, the radiocarbon dates and diagnostic artifacts from Lambert Farm strongly indicate the occurrence of several occupations. It appears that most, if not all, date to the Woodland period in general and possibly the Late Woodland in particular. We will never know precisely how many occupations occurred at this multicomponent site, nor can we determine the dates of each. But we can be certain that Lambert Farm witnessed many episodes of settlement and abandonment by different Native American groups, some of which camped there for several months at a time, while others visited for only a few days.

PATTERNS OF PREHISTORIC ARTIFACTS AND CHIPPING DEBRIS

A common procedure in the analysis of archaeological remains is to identify patterns in various aspects or attributes of the recovered materials, such as their horizontal and vertical distributions, functional and raw material types, and sizes. Once detected, such patterns contribute to understanding the range of human behavior that occurred at the site. This section presents analysis and interpretation of patterns identified in some of the objects from Lambert Farm, namely prehistoric artifacts and chipping debris.

A total of 56,838 cultural remains (both historic and prehistoric) were recovered from all completed sample units at Lambert Farm, including those disturbed by roadway construction and topsoil removal. This amount excludes cultural materials retrieved by flotation, as explained later, since they have not been catalogued. We found prehistoric archaeological remains in all but only 20 of the 523 STPs and all of the 122 EUs. In addition, all of the 13 sample units affected by roadway construction and topsoil removal yielded prehistoric cultural materials, although they are excluded from most of the discussion that follows, unless otherwise noted.

By far, the most commonly recovered prehistoric artifacts from Lambert Farm, as expected, are made of stone. As Table 3.2 indicates, a total of 641 stone artifacts were discovered in the completed units at the site. The vast majority are chipped-stone tools, while the remainder are groundstone objects and hammerstones. The chipped-stone artifacts consist of eight tool types, as listed in Table 3.3. About half of these tools are either projectile points or bifaces. The predominance of these two categories at Lambert Farm, or at any prehistoric site, indicates the occurrence of later stages in stone tool manufacturing or intensive cutting or scraping activities, probably of hard materials resulting in exhaustion and discard (McManamon 1982:8). Similarly, the total 25 incomplete Levanna projectile points were likely discarded due to flaws in the raw material or breakage in manufacturing or use and subsequent unsuccessful attempts at rejuvenation.

Some interesting patterns also emerge from the identification of 14 raw materials of the 641 stone artifacts (Table 3.4). Nearly all these artifacts are made of raw materials that were probably obtained from the immediate or nearby vicinity, within 15 miles or so, of Lambert Farm. Only 27 artifacts are made of exotic raw materials, specifically, hornfels, chert, jasper, and chalcedony. The hornfels most likely originated in the Blue Hills area in Massachusetts, the chert in New York, the jasper in Pennsylvania, and the chalcedony in an unknown source, perhaps as far as Ohio. The majority of stone tools are made of quartz, as are the Levanna projectile points.

TABLE 3.2
STONE ARTIFACT TYPES RECOVERED FROM LAMBERT FARM

Artifact Type	Amount	Percentage
Adze	2	0.3
Atlantic Projectile Point	2	0.3
Axe	2	0.3
Biface	146	22.7
Core[1]	20	3.1
Drill	3	0.5
Fox Creek Projectile Point	1	0.2
Gaming Stone (?)	1	0.2
Hammerstone	7	1.1
Jack's Reef Corner-Notched Projectile Point	1	0.2
Levanna Projectile Point	31	4.8
Madison Projectile Point	3	0.5
Meadowood Projectile Point	1	0.2
Orient Fishtail Projectile Point	5	0.8
Orient Fishtail Projectile Point/Reworked Drill	1	0.2
Preform	83	12.9
Scraper	71	11.0
Small Stemmed Projectile Point	9	1.4
Smoking Pipe	1	0.2
Squibnocket Triangle Projectile Point	2	0.3
Uniface	17	2.6
Untyped Groundstone Tool	1	0.2
Untyped Projectile Point[2]	79	12.3
Untyped Projectile Point/Reworked Scraper	1	0.2
Untyped Stemmed Projectile Point	19	2.9
Untyped Triangle Projectile Point	16	2.5
Wayland Notched Projectile Point	2	0.3
Worked Flake	114	17.8
Total:[3]	641	100.0

[1] Stone artifact from which flakes were removed during stone toolmaking.

[2] Excluding untyped stemmed and untyped triangle projectile points.

[3] Total includes 34 stone artifacts from SF1–6 and SU1–3,5,7,9,10 but excludes 9 ground graphite objects due to difficulty in verifying function.

The seven remaining Levanna projectile points are of other locally available rocks, namely quartzite, felsite, and shale.

Quartz is even more prevalent among the chipping debris, such as flakes, recovered from all completed STPs and EUs. Of the total 29,198 pieces of chipping debris, 27,752 are made of quartz (Table 3.5). The next most commonly recovered raw material is quartzite, accounting for 496 flakes. The eight remaining identified raw materials account for only 950 pieces of chipping debris. Nearly 99% of recovered flakes are made of stones that were probably locally available to the site's residents. Only 340 pieces of chipping debris are made of exotic raw materials, the same materials noted above as well as rhyolite, which probably originated in the Blue Hills area. It is likely that much of the exotic raw material was originally obtained at the quarry or elsewhere away from Lambert Farm by prehistoric Native Americans who did not occupy the site. The Lambert Farm inhabitants could have

TABLE 3.3

CHIPPED-STONE TOOL TYPES RECOVERED FROM LAMBERT FARM

Tool Type	Amount	Percentage
Biface	146	23.3
Core	20	3.2
Drill	3	0.5
Preform	83	13.2
Projectile Point[1]	173	27.6
Scraper	71	11.3
Uniface	17	2.7
Worked Flake	114	18.2
Total:[2]	627	100.0

[1] Includes one projectile point reworked into a drill and one projectile point reworked into a scraper.
[2] Total includes 34 chipped-stone tools from SF1–6 and SU1–3,5,7,9,10.

TABLE 3.4

RAW MATERIAL OF STONE ARTIFACTS RECOVERED FROM LAMBERT FARM

Raw Material	Amount	Percentage
Argillite	18	2.8
Chalcedony	1	0.2
Chert	17	2.6
Cumberlandite	2	0.3
Diorite	2	0.3
Felsite	32	5.0
Granite	2	0.3
Hornfels	5	0.8
Jasper	4	0.6
Quartz	500	78.0
Quartzite	48	7.4
Sandstone	1	0.2
Shale	1	0.2
Steatite	1	0.2
Unidentified	7	1.1
Total:[1]	641	100.0

[1] Total includes 34 stone artifacts from SF1–6 and SU1–3,5,7,9,10 but excludes 9 ground graphite objects due to difficulty in verifying function.

acquired these materials through exchange networks, especially the chert, jasper, and chalcedony that most likely were extracted from sources over 200 miles away. Further, the fact that chipping debris from nonlocal raw materials was discovered at Lambert Farm, albeit in small amounts, indicates that at least some of the stone artifacts made of these exotics were manufactured or resharpened on the site.

Flakes result in great quantities from chipped-stone tool manufacturing and rejuvenation, two activities intensively performed at Lambert Farm. Great amounts of chipping debris occur at prehistoric sites in areas where stone tool production or maintenance took place, as well as where substantial scraping and cutting activities

TABLE 3.5
RAW MATERIAL OF CHIPPING DEBRIS RECOVERED FROM LAMBERT FARM

Raw Material	Amount	Percentage
Argillite	290	1.0
Attleboro Red Felsite	23	0.1
Chalcedony	2	0.1
Chert	137	0.4
Felsite	296	1.0
Hornfels	117	0.4
Jasper	74	0.2
Quartz	27,752	95.0
Quartzite	496	1.6
Rhyolite	10	0.1
Unidentified	1	0.1
Total:[1]	29,198	100.0

[1] Total excludes 2,130 pieces of chipping debris from SF1–6 and SU1–3,5,7,9,10.

TABLE 3.6
SIZE OF CHIPPING DEBRIS RECOVERED FROM LAMBERT FARM

Size[1]	Amount	Percentage
0–1	4,253	14.5
1–3	23,710	81.2
3–5	1,108	3.7
5–7	115	0.4
7–9	11	0.1
11–13	1	0.1
Total:[2]	29,198	100.0

[1] In cm.
[2] Total excludes 2,130 pieces of chipping debris from SF1–6 and SU1–3,5,7,9,10.

resulted in breakage of tools that were subsequently rejuvenated (McManamon 1982:8). As part of the cataloguing procedure, chipping debris recovered from all STPs and EUs was grouped into different categories based on maximum size: 0–1 cm; 1–3 cm; 3–5 cm; 5–7 cm; 7–9 cm; and 11–13 cm (Table 3.6). Some interesting observations are made by comparing the frequencies within each size category. Nearly all flakes are of either the 1–3-cm size or the 0–1-cm size. It should be mentioned, however, that flakes less than the 0.63-cm (0.25-in) mesh size often fell through field screens, and thus their recoveries would not be accurately represented. Flakes with a maximum size of 3 cm tend to result primarily from final shaping and thinning chipped-stone tools and rejuvenating edges blunted by use (McManamon 1982:8). Hence, the extremely high frequency of recovered chipping debris measuring 3 cm or less strongly suggests the predominance of final chipped-stone tool manufacturing or rejuvenation activities at Lambert Farm. The occurrence of primary manufacturing activities in which the initial removal of flakes was performed at the site is indicated by the recovery of 1,235 flakes larger than 3 cm, 20 cores and

TABLE 3.7
DEPTH OF CHIPPING DEBRIS RECOVERED FROM LAMBERT FARM

Depth[1]	Amount	Percentage
0–10	5,902	20.4
10–20	8,500	29.3
20–30	6,196	21.4
30–40	4,054	14.0
40–50	2,101	7.2
50–60	1,203	4.1
60–70	600	2.1
70–80	194	0.7
80–90	141	0.5
90–100	48	0.2
100–110	22	0.1
Total:[2]	28,961	100.0

[1] In 10-cm increments below ground surface.
[2] Total excludes 237 pieces of chipping debris not recovered in 5- or 10-cm levels in EUs and STPs and 2,130 pieces of chipping debris from SF1–6 and SU1–3,5,7,9,10.

seven hammerstones, and an unrecorded number of decortification flakes (i.e., flakes containing their original outer surface).

Only limited interpretations can be made regarding the depth at which prehistoric cultural remains were recovered from Lambert Farm due to a major source of bias: disturbance caused by plowing that occurred at the site during the historic and recent periods. Despite this disturbance, some patterns are still detected from a comparison of the frequencies of chipping debris recovered in 10-cm levels from the STPs and EUs (Table 3.7). The vast majority of the 28,961 flakes were recovered between 0 and 50 cm from ground surface; only 2,208 flakes were found below the 50-cm level, some as deep as 110 cm from ground surface. A nearly identical vertical distribution exists for the 50 projectile points retrieved from 10-cm levels in the STPs and EUs, as 45 projectile points were discovered between 0 and 50 cm from ground surface.

On the other hand, a somewhat different pattern results from comparing the amount (measured in grams) of prehistoric ceramics recovered in 10-cm levels from 29 STPs and 57 EUs, including 21 features (Table 3.8); no prehistoric pottery was found in SF1–6 and SU1–3,5,7,9,10. While just over half of the 1,089.6 gm of prehistoric ceramics were recovered between 0 and 50 cm from ground surface, a relatively large proportion was found below the 50-cm level and as deep as 90 cm from ground surface. Indeed, the two levels containing the second and fourth largest amounts of prehistoric pottery, 70–80-cm level and 50–60-cm level, respectively, account for about one-third of the total prehistoric ceramic weight. The specimens encountered at these two depths were in deep features that extended below the living surfaces of the site. Thus, the depth of these and other remains is misleading when the materials were in such features as pits and burials, since they have been deposited from higher levels into excavated features.

TABLE 3.8
DEPTH OF PREHISTORIC CERAMICS RECOVERED FROM LAMBERT FARM

Depth[1]	Amount[2]	Percentage
0–10	24.3	2.2
10–20	55.7	5.1
20–30	184.8	17.0
30–40	297.2	27.3
40–50	51.9	4.8
50–60	117.9	10.8
60–70	46.5	4.3
70–80	254.1	23.3
80–90	57.2	5.2
Total:[3]	1,089.6	100.0

[1] In 10-cm increments below ground surface.
[2] In gm.
[3] Total excludes 0.3 gm of prehistoric ceramics not recovered in 5- or 10-cm levels.

In addition to studying the frequencies of various types of prehistoric cultural remains unearthed at a site, archaeologists are also interested in examining the spatial patterning of these materials, specifically, their distribution and density. In theory, understanding where certain objects were found and in what amounts is useful in revealing locations within a site where specific activities were performed. For instance, the recovery of relatively great amounts of chipping debris, preforms, and finished stone tools within adjacent sample units indicates the occurrence of stone-tool production and maintenance, perhaps even a lithic workshop. At another location, the presence of prehistoric ceramic sherds within a hearth suggests the occurrence of cooking. The remains of these and other potential activity areas are strewn across Lambert Farm, but determining the extent to which each concentration of materials is spatially and temporally discrete is problematic. Dense accumulations of chipping debris within adjacent sample units could also result from multiple occupations, each associated with limited stone-tool production and maintenance, in addition to a single episode of intense activity associated with a lithic workshop, or even a combination of the two. Distinguishing among these three scenarios is not always possible, due to the operation of factors that may have caused disturbance after the items were originally deposited. These so-called postdepositional processes include (1) erosion, (2) successive occupations during which people and/or animals dug into older remains from earlier levels, (3) plowing, and (4) a combination of these factors (Redman and Watson 1970; Sterud, McManamon, and Rose 1978). Thus, the isolation of spatially and temporally discrete activity areas is much more easily accomplished at small, single-component sites that have not been disturbed, as opposed to large, multicomponent sites that have been plowed, such as Lambert Farm.

In order to demonstrate the difficulty in interpreting the spatial patterning of the Lambert Farm assemblage, let us examine the distribution and densities of different materials. The frequency distributions for projectile points (Figure 3.5), stone artifacts (Figure 3.6), prehistoric ceramics (Figure 3.7), and features (Figure 3.8) are

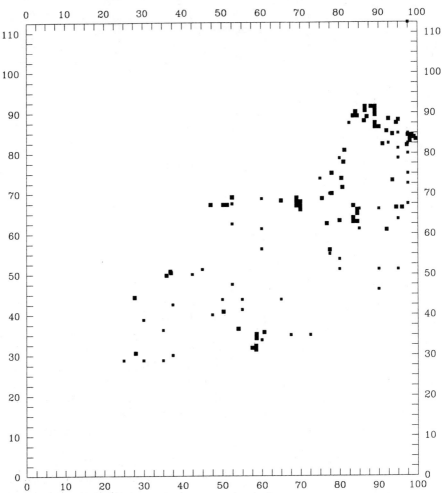

FIGURE 3.5   Distribution of sample units containing projectile points recovered from Lambert Farm.

shown separately. Since chipping debris was recovered in nearly all of the sample units, its frequency distribution is not displayed. Also, it should be emphasized that more features probably existed in the completed sample units than are indicated in Figure 3.8, as features situated within the plow zone were destroyed. It is clear from comparing each of these four figures with Figure 2.4 that not all completed sample units contained projectile points, stone artifacts, prehistoric ceramics, and features. This is not surprising since archaeological sites commonly possess heterogeneous distributions of various types of remains. What is interesting is the tendency of overlapping and clustering exhibited in the figures (the overlapping in Figures 3.5 and 3.6 is due partly to the inclusion of projectile points in the totals of stone artifacts). Many of the sample units that contained stone artifacts, for instance, also contained both prehistoric pottery and features. Further, in most cases a sample unit that con-

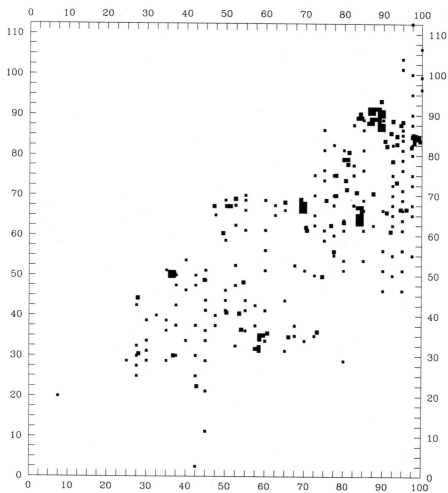

FIGURE 3.6   Distribution of sample units containing stone artifacts recovered from
Lambert Farm.

tained a specific material type is in close proximity (i.e., 2.5–5 m) to another sample
unit that contained the same material. Each of the four figures exhibits relatively
few isolated sample units (i.e., situated beyond 5 m from another sample unit containing the same material). In short, the four figures apparently indicate that different types of material tend to occur together. But it is not that simple.

In drawing attention to these overlapping and clustering patterns of frequency
distribution, I am not arguing that Lambert Farm is unusual in this respect. But
rather I point out that identifying such patterns is one thing and understanding what
they mean is something entirely different, which, in the case of Lambert Farm, is
not at all clear. What is certain, though, is that these and other frequency distributions are an accumulation of different episodes of site use as represented at each
completed sample unit. Due to the disturbances resulting from plowing and multiple

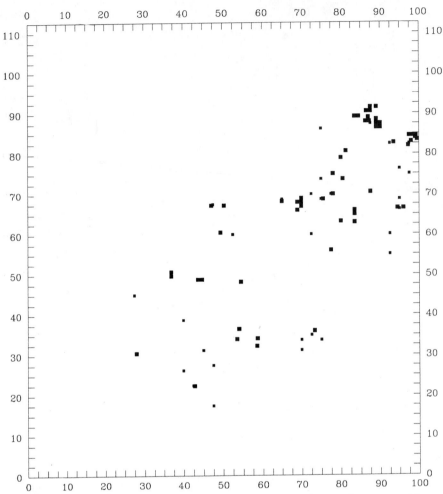

FIGURE 3.7   Distribution of sample units containing prehistoric ceramics recovered from Lambert Farm.

occupations, among other limitations, the creation of frequency distributions for each occupation is simply not possible. We may reasonably assume that the areas utilized at Lambert Farm each time the site was settled in the prehistoric past were not identical. But we are as much unable to pinpoint all of these areas of site use and their respective occupations as we are unable to explain why certain locations may have been favored at Lambert Farm during specific episodes.

Another important limitation of these frequency distributions is that they do not provide information on the varying amounts of prehistoric remains discovered in each unit. Rather, they are based on presence and absence of objects. The distribution of density overcomes this limitation, though it has other shortcomings. Further, using density to plot spatial distribution of recovered materials allows data from different-size units to be comparable. In order to visualize this kind of distribution,

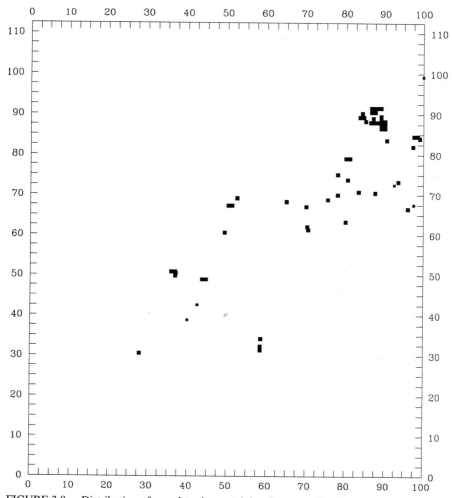

FIGURE 3.8   Distribution of sample units containing features at Lambert Farm.

we assigned density values for various types of prehistoric remains. For illustrative purposes, only density of projectile points and prehistoric ceramics are discussed here. Every completed STP and EU received a density value; units SF1–6 and SU1–3,5,7,9,10 were excluded because of prior disturbance. These values were calculated by totalling the frequency of projectile points, and by totalling the number of grams for prehistoric ceramics, from each unit and dividing the sum by the area (m²) of the unit; area (m²), as opposed to volume (m³), of each unit was used to calculate density values since unit depth was affected by previous disturbance to the site. Hence, two projectile points recovered from a 50 × 50-cm STP received a density value of 8 per m². Density of prehistoric ceramics is based on sherd weight rather than sherd frequency because the former is a more accurate representation. For instance, if sherd frequency were used to calculate density, a unit containing 50 sherds weighing a combined 2 gm would possess a significantly higher density value

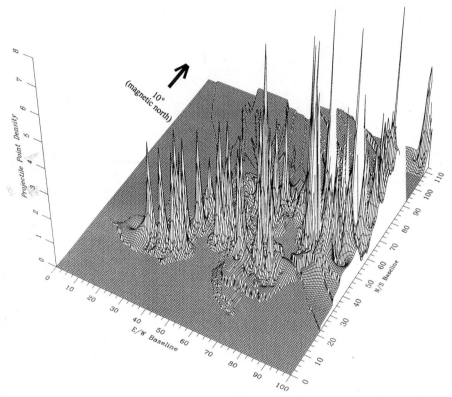

FIGURE 3.9   Three-dimensional plot of density of projectile points recovered per m² from Lambert Farm.

than another sample unit of the same size containing only three sherds weighing a total 30 gm. The use of sherd weight, on the other hand, provides a less biased value of density since it is not directly based on the vagaries of vessel breakage; in the prior example the use of sherd weight to calculate density indicates more reliably that the latter sample unit would possess a much higher density figure than that of the former sample unit. Density values for projectile points that included a fraction were rounded down to the whole integer, except when less than a value of 1, in which case it was rounded up to the value of 1. Density values for ceramics were calculated to two decimal points but were not rounded up or down.

After all density values were calculated for every completed STP and EU, the information was input into a computer software program (SURFER, Version 4, published by Golden Software, Inc.). This sophisticated mapping program produced three-dimensional contour maps depicting the spatial distribution patterns of projectile points (Figure 3.9) and prehistoric ceramics (Figure 3.10) as expressed by density per square meter excavated at each unit. The value of computer-generated contour maps is primarily in their effectiveness in providing a visual presentation of spatial distribution patterns that otherwise may not be as apparent (Haigh and Kelly 1987). Looking at Figures 3.9 and 3.10, one is immediately confronted with a vast

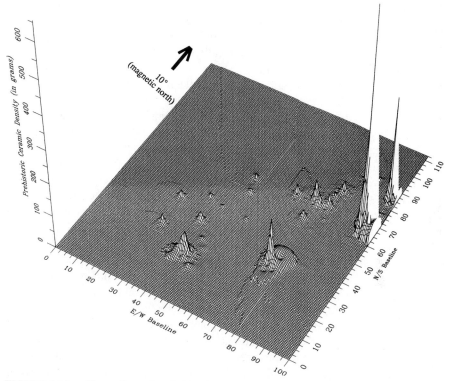

FIGURE 3.10   Three-dimensional plot of density of prehistoric ceramics recovered (in gm) per m² from Lambert Farm.

array of surfaces depicting peaks, valleys, plateaus, and low-lying planes that correspond to different levels of density of either projectile points or prehistoric ceramics recovered per square meter from each unit. Such a visual presentation of spatial distribution enables the identification of gaps and clusters of relatively high and low densities of the two material types excavated at Lambert Farm.

The purpose of displaying Figures 3.9 and 3.10 is to stress the complexity and difficulty in interpreting density distribution patterns at multicomponent sites that have been plowed, such as Lambert Farm, despite the clear presentation of such patterns. First, both of these figures must be viewed with caution, since some, if not all, of the patterns may be misleading for various reasons. Both maps project values for areas between completed units that were not tested. In both cases the SURFER program, as is typical of computer contouring software, interpolated density values based on actual values from surrounding completed units. The result is that these untested spaces were assigned interpolated density values that appear as various surfaces, such as peaks, indicating relatively high density values, or low-density flat surfaces, indicating a value of zero. This may be overcome, to some extent, by examining the surface displayed only at the completed units in each map. Another limitation of both density distribution maps is the problem of representativeness of the data. It is not possible to determine the extent to which the recovered information is representative of the original density (and frequency) distribution patterns. This is due to the completion of STP transects only in the more productive areas of the site and the systematic (i.e., biased) selection of EU locations. High-density areas were sampled preferentially as necessitated by time and funding constraints, as well as by an explicit research design that sought to maximize the recovery of prehistoric cultural remains prior to their imminent destruction by residential development.

Lastly, and perhaps most important, is the problem that is also inherent in the frequency distribution maps—the information displayed at each completed sample unit is not necessarily temporally distinct but represents an amalgamation of different episodes of prehistoric human use of Lambert Farm. The frequency and density distribution maps are based on the total, not subtotal, of specific remains at each sample unit that span, not distinguish among, different times when the site was inhabited. In short, these maps are limited to depicting locations across Lambert Farm at which varying amounts of remains were deposited during all periods of settlement. This is primarily a result of stratigraphic contamination caused by multiple occupations and plowing. Besides breaking fragile materials, including stone tools, plowing at an archaeological site destroys the original provenience of cultural materials within the plow zone, rendering their precise horizontal and vertical locations unknowable. A few studies have furthered our understanding of the far-reaching effects of plowing at sites (Hoffman 1982; Redman and Watson 1970; Roper 1976; Sterud, McManamon, and Rose 1978; and Trubowitz 1978). Roper's (1976:372–74) study, which involved comparing measurements of displaced biface sections at the plowed Airport site in Springfield, Illinois, concludes that the lateral disturbance caused by plowing may not necessarily be as severe as is often thought. This project and others have shown that the relative horizontal associations among plowed cultural materials remain constant if plowing is done in a back-and-forth manner, as opposed to cross-cutting and intersecting (Sterud, McManamon, and Rose 1978:102). For instance, while a concentration of remains situated within 30 cm below ground surface is laterally displaced by back-and-forth plowing, the original concentration is still discernible, assuming that other disturbances are at a minimum. In other words, artifacts will shift from their original places of deposition, but all artifacts will remain in, approximately, the same relationship to one another if the pattern of plowing occurs in a back-and-forth motion.

At Lambert Farm, the plowing pattern was not detected, and there is no reason to assume that plowing was done only in a back-and-forth manner. Nevertheless, it is possible that the frequency and density distribution patterns are accurately depicted in a relative manner, just somewhat laterally displaced from their original locations. But even if the relative horizontal relationship among objects in the plow zone remained constant, the plowing permanently altered the temporal association among these materials through vertical mixing. This lack of stratigraphic control is a major reason why correlating all the materials recovered in each sample unit with their specific occupations is not possible and, thus, why the frequency and density distribution patterns of the Lambert Farm assemblage are based on an accumulation of different episodes of site use represented at each completed sample unit. In sum, while spatially and temporally discrete occupation areas undoubtedly occurred at

Lambert Farm, their identification is seriously hampered by the disruptive effects of multiple occupations and plowing.

SUBSISTENCE AND SEASONALITY

In addition to the prehistoric artifacts and chipping debris, abundant and diverse, well-preserved animal and plant remains were discovered at Lambert Farm. The majority of these resources were encountered within features consisting of relatively dense shell deposits. Not all of the identified faunal material, however, represent food residue, as elaborated in the next chapter. In any case, based on the recovery of shells, bones, teeth, nutshells, and seeds, it is clear that the people who settled at Lambert Farm relied on locally available resources to maintain a rich and varied diet.

Shell deposits seem ubiquitous at the site. Their diversity and distribution are discussed in the next chapter. But related and puzzling questions have remained largely unanswered since the surprising discovery of especially dense shell deposits at Lambert Farm in 1988: Why did the prehistoric Native Americans who inhabited the site transport such huge quantities of shells, in excess of several hundred pounds, about one mile uphill to this location? Why didn't they leave all the shells at the shore and carry only the extracted, and thus exceedingly lighter, shellfish meat to the site? And why didn't the Native Americans of Lambert Farm settle instead along the shore to procure, process, and consume all the shellfish?

Features 2 and 22, which contained great amounts of shellfish remains and the three dog burials, may hold some clues. But it is practically impossible to address these questions without knowing whether or not the densities of shellfish remains at Lambert Farm varied over time. Although this information is unknown, the limited (and thus likely biased) results of radiocarbon dating of shell samples from the site provide some insight. It appears that shellfish were intensively gathered and transported to Lambert Farm beginning perhaps as early as 1280 B.P. until at least 490 B.P., based on the calibrated dates. Presuming that people were also present at Lambert Farm between at least 3000 and 1280 B.P. (ca. 1000 B.C. and A.D. 670), as indicated by recovered diagnostic artifacts, shellfish may have played a lesser role in the diet of the site's inhabitants during this time for reasons currently unknown. Perhaps limited access to coastal resources due to increased population pressure and territoriality in the coastal zone sometime after 1280 B.P. prevented some groups from residing along shore. This hypothesis needs further developing and testing by future research, but it is clear that people who resided at sites situated within walkable distance to the coast, such as Lambert Farm, were still able to collect shellfish and transport them back to their habitation sites.

It is also clear that the Native American inhabitants of Lambert Farm likely ate much more shellfish than represented by the discovered and undiscovered shellfish remains at the site. They could have consumed a relatively large amount and wide variety of molluscs along the shore each time they gathered shellfish. A similar argument was made by Quilter and Stocker (1983), who excavated the Paloma site, which is located near the central coast of Peru on the northern edge of the Chilca

Valley about 2.8 miles (4.5 km) from the Pacific shore. Despite its size (5 ha), age (about 7200–4800 B.P., 5200–2800 B.C.), and other differences, this noncoastal site shares some striking similarities with Lambert Farm, as it contains dense shell midden concentrations, some over 1 meter thick. Quilter and Stocker (1983:550) maintain that the shell deposits at the site may underrepresent the amount of seafood eaten by the Palomans:

> As the site is a long uphill walk from the shore, it is curious that the site inhabitants took the trouble to haul both shell and meat to the site when processing on the shore could have considerably lightened their burden. Numerous grass-lined pits at Paloma may be evidence of short-term storage. Judging from the size of the pits, a maximum of from five to six dozen mussels could have been stored at any one time in each pit. Of course, the primary storage area for shellfish was the beaches and rocks where they thrive. Any storage pits at Paloma were there for convenience, to be used by less-mobile villagers or groups engaged in other subsistence pursuits. . . . Thus, consumption at or near the collection site, processing at the beach for later use, and short-term storage at Paloma may be factors that have produced an underrepresentation of seafood in shell middens.

It should be pointed out here that close to Lambert Farm are two prehistoric sites that also contained some shellfish remains. At the Macera I site, located approximately .7 mile (1.1 km) southwest of Lambert Farm and about 1.2 miles (1.9 km) west of Greenwich Bay, as shown in Figure 1.2, limited testing uncovered low-density shellfish deposits (Morenon 1981). The age of the site is unknown as no radiocarbon dates were obtained, nor were any diagnostic artifacts found; the recovery of prehistoric ceramics, however, indicates that Macera I was at least affiliated with the Woodland period. Situated just .25 mile (.4 km) east of Macera I, approximately .5 mile (.85 km) south of Lambert Farm and almost 1 mile (1.5 km) west of Greenwich Bay, is Macera II (see Figure 1.2). At this site the remains of quahogs, oysters, and scallops were recovered in a shell midden. Based on two corrected radiocarbon dates (4,930 ± 160 B.P. [ca. 3000 B.C.] obtained from charcoal in a hearth not associated with the midden and 350 ± 100 B.P. obtained from quahog shells from the midden), the site was utilized at least during the Late Archaic and Late Woodland periods (Morenon 1981). Unfortunately, Macera II was heavily disturbed by artifact looters, thus seriously compromising its interpretive value. The relationship, if any, of these two sites with Lambert Farm is not known. Also, dog burials were not recovered at either Macera I or II.

Returning to the shell deposits at Lambert Farm, it is difficult to prove who collected the shellfish. We can speculate that special-purpose task groups walked the path regularly to the shore to gather clams. They most likely frequented Greenwich Bay and vicinity, as this was the closest coastal setting and it supported the various shellfish remains found at the site. We can speculate further that these task groups consisted largely of women and children. Ethnographic accounts of coastal hunter-gatherers support such a division of labor based on sex and age. In any case, the people who gathered the shellfish were probably assisted by others in transporting the shells and the extracted meat in baskets to Lambert Farm, given the heavy weight of many shells and the arduous uphill hike back to the site.

Although the location of Lambert Farm was not as convenient for the procurement of shellfish as it would have been at the shore, it was possibly more conve-

TABLE 3.9
NUMBER OF IDENTIFIED SPECIMENS (NISP) FOR SPECIES IN LAMBERT FARM VERTEBRATE ASSEMBLAGE (GEORGE 1993)

es	NISP	Percentage
ite-Tailed Deer (Odocoileus virginianus)	255	67.1
Dog/Wolf/Coyote[1] (Canis, sp.)	31	8.1
Moose (Alces americana)	2	0.5
Raccoon (Procyon lotor)	1	0.3
Muskrat (Ondatra zibethica)	1	0.3
Total Mammals:	290	76.3
Tautog (Tautoga onitus)	25	6.6
Atlantic Sturgeon (Acipenser oxyrhynchus)	15	4.0
Atlantic Cod (Gadus morhua)	2	0.5
Shark[1]	2	0.5
Total Fish:	44	11.6
Box Turtle (Terrapene carolina)	30	7.9
Total Reptiles:	30	7.9
Wild Turkey (Meleagris gallopavo)	13	3.4
Duck[1] (Bucephala, sp.)	3	0.8
Total Birds:	16	4.2
Total NISP:	380	100.0

[1] Species-level identification could not be made.

In any event, there is considerable archaeological evidence from other sites in the Northeast and around the world that prehistoric dogs were eaten by people, in addition to having been buried, either alone or in human graves. Among the earliest accounts in the Northeast is an article written in 1868 by Wyman. The author reported that at Mount Desert in Maine and at two sites in Massachusetts, Eagle Hill in Ipswich and Cotuit Port in Barnstable on Cape Cod, broken dog bones were found with bones of other edible animals. Wyman (1868:576) concluded that these disarticulated dog remains represented meals consumed by the sites' Native American residents. Similarly, in 1898 Eaton wrote about "ancient shell-heaps" on Block Island, off the Rhode Island coast. Three of these features contained shafts of limb bones of dogs that Eaton (1898:147) believed were intentionally broken to extract

nient for the hunting of animals and gathering of pl̸
Of course, freshwater first had to be present in c̸
be inhabited, since water is difficult to carry and ̸
on a daily basis, than food. The freshwater spring
Farm likely existed during Native American settlemeı.
location of Lambert Farm may have been less the resu̸
place along the coast and more related to a deliberate atteṇ̸
occupied to exploit a greater range of food resources than ma)
the shore alone. The abundant and diverse subsistence remains
bert Farm is the subject of the remainder of the chapter.

In addition to the shellfish remains, numerous specimens of pṛ
and teeth were recovered from Lambert Farm, including the remains ̸
that were found articulated in burials, meaning that they were in their propͺ
ical position as if still connected to tissue. The vast majority of faunal remą
encountered within 38 shell deposits, having been preserved by these features.

A small sample of exceptionally well-preserved vertebrate faunal material, o̸
mains of animals with backbones, was analyzed by George (1993) of the Universıͺ
of Connecticut at Storrs. The sample consisted of 380 disarticulated specimens recovered from 14 prehistoric features within 24 units; the articulated skeletal remains
of the three dogs were examined separately and are discussed in the next chapter.
Using comparative osteological collections of southern New England fauna, George
attempted to complete the following steps: identification to the most detailed taxonomic level possible, preferably species; identification and analysis of butchery
marks; identification and description of seasonally sensitive fauna (e.g., white-tailed
deer, anadromous fish, and migratory waterfowl); and determination of the level of
maturity. Table 3.9 lists the number of identified specimens (NISP) for each species
in the analyzed Lambert Farm vertebrate assemblage. It should be made clear, however, that most of the recovered prehistoric bone and tooth remains were not examined due to funding constraints, and thus it is possible, if not likely, that the remains
of additional animal species not included in Table 3.9 were also recovered from the
site. Nevertheless, the results of George's analysis, as summarized next, provide
considerable data on the diet of the Native American residents at Lambert Farm.

White-tailed deer is by far the most abundant species represented in the sample.
Further, these remains were discovered in all 14 features and 24 sample units and
nearly all 62 levels analyzed. Diversity in the white-tailed deer skeletal elements indicates that these animals were butchered at Lambert Farm. Species of the genus
Canis (i.e., dogs, wolves, and coyotes) are the second most abundant animal represented in the assemblage. This comes somewhat as a surprise since the three dog
burials were not included in George's analysis. All the canid remains in this sample
were disarticulated. They were discovered in 10 of the analyzed sample units (8 features), but due to their fragmentary condition, it was not possible to identify whether
these remains were of dog, wolf, or coyote. Nevertheless, it is striking that in addition to the burying of three dogs, other dogs were possibly being consumed at Lambert Farm, though not necessarily during the same periods of settlement in which
the three dogs were interred. It is conceivable, however, that some of the disarticulated dog bones were broken and displaced from burials due to plowing and other
disturbances to subsurface deposits at the site.

marrow. More recently, Luedtke (1980) excavated the remains of a relatively small adult dog from Calf Island, a Late Woodland site in Boston Harbor. Many cut marks on most of the dog's bones convinced her that the animal had been butchered. Luedtke (1980:61) also reasoned that the frequent cut marks on the carpals and phalanges, or foot and toe bones, in particular, suggested that the dog was skinned and then probably disjointed. Its vertebral column, or backbone, was found articulated and off to one side of the shell midden from which the butchered bones were recovered.

Moose remains, which are not common at southern New England prehistoric sites, are represented at Lambert Farm by two vertebrae specimens (from EU 3 Feature 2 and EU 51 Feature 19). It is likely that the butchering of one or two moose occurred at the location of the kill(s), rather than at Lambert Farm, given the difficulty in transporting such a large animal; this may also explain the relatively low total count of moose elements in the sample. On the other hand, the recovery of tautog teeth and dental plates suggests that these fish were processed at Lambert Farm.

Identified butchery marks are rare, occurring on just three white-tailed deer bones in the sample (from EU 8 Feature 2, EU 38 Feature 15, and EU 69 Feature 19). In each case George observed the cut marks on and around articular joints, apparently the result of slicing with stone tools, as opposed to chopping or sawing. Despite the few butchery marks, we can presume that the identified disarticulated, non-canid bones and teeth most likely represent consumed meals, though some of these remains were also fashioned into tools. Curiously, only a few specimens in the sample exhibit signs of having been burned. This may indicate that some of the raw meat was dried after the animals were butchered, while other meat remained on the bone when it was cooked at relatively low temperatures that did not burn the analyzed specimens. None of the identified bones show carnivore gnaw marks.

In order to assist in reconstructing subsistence and seasonality, recovered floral or paleobotanical remains were also examined. These specimens, which may include charred seeds, nutshells, and wild and domesticated plants (e.g., maize, beans, and squash), tend to be so small that they are not usually recovered in the sifting screens. Thus, 70 soil samples were taken from various features at Lambert Farm so that any paleobotanical remains contained in these samples could be extracted separately. This was accomplished by PAL staff, directed by Donna Raymond, laboratory supervisor at PAL, using water flotation, a technique standardly employed to recover plant macrofossils from archaeological contexts (Watson 1976). Flotation was performed using the Model A Flote-Tech machine, which incorporated aeration into the water. This machine has a 100-gallon water tank and a maximum pumping rate of 60 gallons per minute. The contents of each soil sample were emptied separately into the water tank. Materials from each sample were recovered within a heavy (1.6-mm mesh) and a light (0.33-mm mesh) sieve or fraction. Once the recovered materials dried, they were sorted using both a magnifier and a stereomicroscope in order to separate paleobotanical specimens for subsequent identification; all cultural materials, including seeds, nutshells, chipping debris, bones, and ceramics, recovered from flotation have not yet been catalogued.

Following the completion of flotation processing and initial sorting by PAL staff, the separated paleobotanical specimens from only four features were identified (due to funding constraints) to the most detailed taxonomic level possible by

Table 3.10
Taxa and Provenience of Identified Charred Seed and Nutshell Remains Recovered from Flotation Samples of Four Analyzed Features at Lambert Farm (Largy 1994)

Feature	Unit	Depth[1]	Seed[2]	Nutshell[2]
2	EU 3	45	Gramineae[3] family (1)	Carya[4], sp. (6)
			Paniceae[5] tribe (1)	cf.[6] Quercus[7], sp. (11)
		57	Gramineae family (2)	cf. Quercus, sp. (5)
				Carya, sp. (12)
				cf. Carya, sp. (10)
		60–65	Rubus[8], sp. (1)	Carya, sp. (16)
			cf. Phytolacca[9] (1)	cf. Carya, sp. (1)
			cf. Polygonaceae[10] family (1)	cf. Quercus, sp. (9)
		90–100	Solanaceae[11] family (1)	
			cf. Paniceae tribe (1)	
	EU 8	25–30		Carya, sp. (1)
				cf. Quercus, sp. (8)
		30–40		Carya, sp. (32)
				cf. Quercus, sp. (1)
		50–60	Cyperaceae[12] family (1)	Quercus, sp. (1)
				cf. Quercus, sp. (13)
				Carya, sp. (1)
		60–70	Paniceae tribe (3)	Carya, sp. (1)
			cf. Vaccinium[13], sp. (1)	cf. Carya, sp. (14)
				cf. Quercus, sp. (19)
		73	Chenopodium[14], sp. (1)	Carya, sp. (4)
			cf. Vaccinium, sp. (3)	cf. Quercus, sp. (1)
		70–80	cf. Vaccinium, sp. (1)	Carya, sp. (15)
				Quercus, sp. (9)
		80–90		Carya, sp. (2)
				Quercus, sp. (3)
		100–110		Carya, sp. (4)
				Quercus, sp. (4)
	Subtotal:		19	203
15	EU 38	40–65		cf. Quercus, sp. (1)
		70–75		Carya, sp. (2)
				Quercus, sp. (16)
		90–95		Carya, sp. (3)
				Quercus, sp. (2)
				cf. Quercus, sp. (1)
	Subtotal:		0	25

(continued)

Largy (1994), a consulting paleobotanist. In addition, other paleobotanical specimens from the four features were identified by Largy using a stereomicroscope to
analyze completely all light-fraction and several heavy-fraction samples from the
four features; those heavy-fraction samples that were not examined entirely were
scanned visually or subsampled. A total of 45 flotation samples from Features 2, 15,
16, and 22 were analyzed by Largy, who focused on the identification of charred

TABLE 3.10 *(continued)*

Feature	Unit	Depth[1]	Seed[2]	Nutshell[2]
16	EU 39	45–50		*Carya*, sp. (4)
				Quercus, sp. (3)
		60–70	*Rubus*, sp. (1)	cf. *Quercus*, sp. (1)
		85–90	Solanaceae family (2)	cf. *Quercus*, sp. (3)
			Rubus, sp. (1)	cf. *Carya*, sp. (2)
	EU 40	60–65	*Rubus*, sp. (2)	cf. *Quercus*, sp. (5)
		75–80	*Gaylusaccia*[15], sp. (1)	*Carya*, sp. (1)
			Paniceae tribe (1)	cf. *Quercus*, sp. (1)
			cf. Cyperaceae family (1)	
	Subtotal:		9	20
22	EU 64	10–20	*Cornus* [*amomum*][16] (1)	
			cf. *Crataegus*[17], sp. (3)	
		20–30	cf. *Crataegus*, sp. (3)	*Carya*, sp. (6)
				cf. *Carya*, sp. (4)
				cf. *Quercus*, sp. (4)
		30–40		*Carya*, sp. (11)
				Quercus, sp. (3)
		40–50	*Gaylussacia*, sp. (1)	*Carya*, sp. (3)
				cf. *Quercus*, sp. (6)
		50–60	*Rubus*, sp. (1)	cf. *Carya*, sp. (1)
			cf. *Crataegus*, sp. (1)	
		60–70	*Gaylussacia*, sp. (1)	
		70–80		cf. *Quercus*, sp. (2)
				Carya, sp. (5)
	Subtotal:		11	45
Total Number of Specimens:			39	293

[1] In cm.
[2] Quantity of specimens in parentheses.
[3] Grass.
[4] Hickory.
[5] Millet.
[6] Specimen closely resembles particular species or genus as definite identification could not be made.
[7] Acorn.
[8] Blackberry, raspberry, dewberry.
[9] Pokeweed.
[10] Buckwheat.
[11] Nightshade.
[12] Sedge.
[13] Blueberry.
[14] Goosefoot, lambsquarter.
[15] Huckleberry.
[16] Silky dogwood.
[17] Hawthorn.

(carbonized) specimens. Table 3.10 lists the 39 identified charred seed and 293 charred nutshell remains recovered from flotation samples from the four features. The results of Largy's analysis are highlighted next.

Many prehistoric Native American groups greatly relied on wild plants as an important part of their subsistence. Nutshells and carbonized seeds from fruits and berries are the most common floral remains preserved by accidentally falling into a hearth during food preparation or by disposal of food remains from a meal. It should be stressed, however, that these same specimens might have no cultural association as they could have been carbonized by blowing into a fire or by being charred in a generalized natural or cultural "burn" over an area (Largy 1994). While uncharred floral remains from Lambert Farm were recovered by flotation, their uncharred condition makes it difficult to determine whether they represent food remains.

A total of 39 charred seeds and/or seed fragments were identified from Features 2, 16, and 22. Feature 2 contained 19 identified carbonized seeds, all of which were recovered in various levels below 45 cm from ground surface. Seven of these seeds were identified as the Gramineae family, including four seeds of the Paniceae tribe. It is possible that several of the unidentified seeds from this feature also belong to this family. Grass seeds are edible, and charred millet seeds have been identified in several prehistoric sites in southern New England and eastern New York.

Feature 16 contained 9 identified carbonized seeds, of which 4 are *Rubus,* sp. Charred seeds of this genus are commonly found at prehistoric sites in New England. *Rubus* includes blackberries, raspberries, and dewberries, which are rich in vitamin C and potassium and can be eaten fresh or dried and pounded into cakes. The seeds grow along edges of fields, clearings, and woodlands. The single carbonized seed of *Gaylussacia,* sp., in the feature represents one of the most commonly identified plant remains in southern New England prehistoric sites. Huckleberry shrubs grow in dry, open oak forests, and both the shrub and the fruit resemble the blueberry.

Feature 22 contained 11 identified charred seeds, of which one is *Cornus [amomum]*. Silky dogwood, a common shrub of moist thickets, produces berries that are not edible by humans. Species of this genus, however, have been used for other purposes. For example, Densmore (1928, 1929:45) reported that during historic times the Chippewa used the bark of *C. stolonifera* and *C. rugosa* as smoking materials and for medicine and dye. Also among the charred seeds recovered from Feature 22 was one nearly complete nutlet and six fragments most resembling *Crataegus,* sp. The hawthorn is a small tree that grows in open clearings and bears an edible red berry. According to Elias and Dykeman (1982:237), "the fruits were used by Indians to some extent in pemmican" during the historic period.

A total of 293 carbonized nutshell fragments identified as *Quercus,* sp. (acorn), and *Carya,* sp. (hickory), were recovered from the flotation samples of the four analyzed features. The specimens are generally very small, ranging in size from 0.3 cm to 0.5 cm, and smaller fragments that are probably these species are identified as "cf.," meaning they closely resemble a particular species but definite identification could not be made (Table 3.10). In addition, the following 9 charred nutshell fragments, all of *Carya,* sp., and all from Feature 13, were recovered in field screens and previously identified by Largy (1989): 4 fragments from EU 34, 30–40 cm below ground surface; 4 fragments from EU 34, 40–50 cm below ground surface; and 1 fragment from STP T39-82.5, 80–90 cm below ground surface. Both acorns and hickory nuts were ingredients in meat stews and breads made by Native Americans during at least historic times.

One class of floral remains noticeably absent from Table 3.10 is domesticated crops such as corn, beans, and squash. While it is possible that these botanical remains were present at Lambert Farm but simply were not recovered or have not yet been identified in the nonanalyzed flotation samples, their apparent absence is consistent with the majority of Woodland sites in the Narragansett Bay area in particular and coastal southern New England in general. Unlike many areas of western and southern portions of the Northeast and elsewhere in eastern North America, domesticated plants in coastal southern New England, with few exceptions, were not a significant part of prehistoric diets. For the Narragansett Bay area, this contradicts ethnohistorical observations of extensive horticulture reported in the mid–seventeenth century (Williams 1973). Ceci (1979, 1990) has hypothesized that Native American plant domestication became an intensive subsistence activity throughout coastal southern New England and coastal New York in response to European contact.

Whether or not horticulture was practiced by the people at Lambert Farm during the Woodland period, it is conceivable that the area surrounding the site for much, if not all, of its occupations was cleared of trees. If domesticated crops were grown at or near the site, trees would have been cut and/or burned to create fields for planting. In the absence of, or in addition to, horticulture during the prehistoric and contact periods, land was still cleared to facilitate hunting by creating an open forest, by driving game with fire, and by attracting animals (especially deer) with new growth (Bernstein 1993:125). Also, the cutting of trees would have provided an important source of firewood, which was constantly in demand.

Evidence of land clearing within the Narragansett Bay area during the prehistoric and contact periods exists in the form of ethnohistorical records and pollen grains. During his visit to Narragansett Bay in 1524, Verrazzano noted expansive treeless stretches of land for miles along the bay (Wroth 1970, cited in Bernstein 1993:124–25). Native American land clearing that occurred prior to European contact is indicated by pollen taken from sediment at the bottom of various lakes and ponds not far from Lambert Farm. This includes the following: pollen dating to before the contact period from Goddard Lake near the Greenwich Cove site, about 5 km southeast of Lambert Farm (Bernstein 1993:124); pollen dating to ca. 850 B.P. from Pasacaco Pond, about 20 km southeast of Lambert Farm (Bernabo 1977, cited in Bernstein 1993:124); and pollen dating to ca. 750 B.P. near the Campbell site, about 20 km southeast of Lambert Farm (Thorbahn and Cox 1988:172, cited in Bernstein 1993:124). Prehistoric pollen sequences from these locations indicate a decrease in tree pollen and an increase in plants (particularly ragweed [*Ambrosia*, sp.]) characteristic of disturbed soils (Bernstein 1993:124). Land clearing at these prehistoric areas and any others at which it may have occurred, including Lambert Farm and vicinity, does not necessarily mean that horticulture was also practiced.

Evidence of specific seasons in which prehistoric human settlement occurred, referred to as seasonality, is often based on the identification of the season of death of fauna and flora whose remains are recovered at a site. In addition, the identification of the time of year during which an animal or plant is maximally available also is used to reconstruct seasonality if the remains of the particular organism are found at the site. For instance, migratory waterfowl such as geese, anadromous fish such as salmon, and nuts such as hickory are present in especially large numbers in certain environmental settings during specific times of the year. Finding abundant remains of these resources at a site might indicate seasonality, though seasonal availability can fluctuate. This approach is less reliable than the use of season of death and, as such, offers only general estimates of seasonality. Even if precise seasons of death or availability of recovered faunal and floral remains are identified, however, it does not necessarily mean that these foods were consumed during the same seasons and that settlement was limited to these seasons. Clearly, some foods were stored and eaten an indeterminable number of weeks or months following the kill or harvest. Similarly, just because a food resource was maximally available during a particular season, it still may have been obtained or eaten during a different (and often unknown) time of year.

In light of these interpretive limitations, seasonality reconstructions can be made from certain shellfish, bone, tooth, nutshell, and seed remains recovered from Lambert Farm (Table 3.11). Annual and daily growth increments are preserved in the shells of various molluscs, including quahogs (Kennish 1980). During the winter when shell growth is very slow in the Northeast, a dark, translucent layer of calcium carbonate forms on the outer edge and inside of the quahog. During rapid periods of growth, between spring and late summer in the Northeast, the deposited shell material is opaque. It is possible to infer the season and even the month of death of a quahog by sectioning the shell, identifying the presence of a translucent or opaque band on the shell's margin, counting the microscopic daily growth lines in the outermost layers of the last annual increment, and comparing the observed growth pattern to a reference collection of modern quahog specimens whose time of death is known.

A preliminary seasonality study involving the sectioning of 98 quahog shell specimens recovered from eight prehistoric features (2, 4, 15, 19, 21, 22, 26, and 34) at Lambert Farm was performed by Greenspan (1990), former laboratory director at PAL, in order to identify the season of death of each specimen and presumably the associated season(s) of prehistoric human occupation at the site. The analysis involved embedding the shell specimens in fiberglass resin and cross-sectioning them using a rock saw; laboratory facilities at the Geology Department, University of Rhode Island, were made available for this preparation. The specimens were then hand-polished so that seasonal growth bands could be examined under a dissecting microscope. Modern quahog specimens previously collected from Greenwich Cove by Bernstein (1987) was used as a reference to develop a model of seasonal growth for quahog in Narragansett Bay. The results of this study indicate that each of the eight analyzed features contained shells that were collected during more than one season. In fact, six features (2, 15, 21, 22, 26, and 34) contained shells that were gathered during all four seasons of the year (Greenspan 1990). If this unexpected, though tentative, conclusion is accurate and is supported by additional shellfish seasonality analysis proposed by PAL, then each of the eight features may have been utilized during multiple seasonal episodes.

Seasonality information is also available from some of the recovered disarticulated vertebrate remains identified by George (1993). Maturity levels of white-tailed deer in the analyzed Lambert Farm assemblage range from juvenile to young to older adult. Since deer usually give birth in May or June (Cronan 1968:121; Hamilton and Whitaker 1979:320), the examined juvenile remains indicate a summer

TABLE 3.11
SEASONALITY RECONSTRUCTION BASED ON ANALYZED FAUNAL AND FLORAL REMAINS RECOVERED FROM LAMBERT FARM[1]

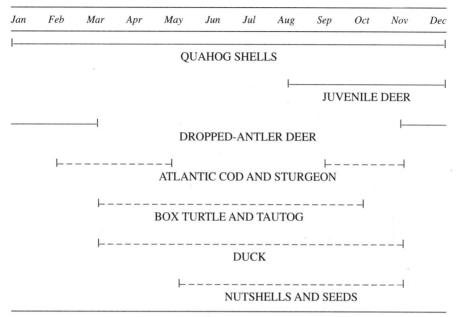

Jan	Feb	Mar	Apr	May	Jun	Jul	Aug	Sep	Oct	Nov	Dec

QUAHOG SHELLS

JUVENILE DEER

DROPPED-ANTLER DEER

ATLANTIC COD AND STURGEON

BOX TURTLE AND TAUTOG

DUCK

NUTSHELLS AND SEEDS

[1] ⊢——⊣ refers to season of death; ⊢ – –⊣ refers to season of maximum availability.

and/or fall season of death, and the season of death for the identified young adult remains is likely fall. A late fall and/or winter season of death is supported by some of the other analyzed deer bones, specifically, those from which antlers had recently dropped prior to the kill. Deer usually shed their antlers during this time of year (Hamilton and Whitaker 1979:319). In addition, the size of the antlers from the remains of one deer (from EU 80 Feature 34), which had not yet been shed, suggests that this animal died during the fall or early winter (George 1993). Although the assemblage also contains dropped antlers, seasonality estimates of these remains are not reliable, since antlers may have been retrieved over a wider time period than when they were naturally detached from the skull. Some of the detached antlers found at Lambert Farm were used to produce chipped-stone tools, based on patterns of wear on the ends of the antlers.

Winter is also estimated as the season of death for the two recovered moose specimens since, according to ethnohistorical observations (DeForest 1852:207; Josselyn 1988:98), moose were primarily hunted by Native Americans during the winter season once the deep snows had fallen so that the hunters could track the animal. Seasons of death for other fauna identified in the vertebrate assemblage are estimated (though by no means definitive) on the basis of maximum periods of availability and additional ethnohistorical documentation (DeForest 1852; Josselyn 1988; Williams 1973; Wood 1977): Atlantic cod and Atlantic sturgeon (spring or fall); box turtle and tautog (late spring–early fall); and duck (spring–fall). Thus, seasonality estimates of the analyzed vertebrate sample indicate that Lambert Farm may have been occupied on a year-round basis and/or during different seasons of successive years (George 1993). It should be pointed out that the dashed lines in Table 3.11, which represent seasons of maximum availability of certain organisms, tend to distort the seasonality reconstruction of the site. This is not only due to the likelihood that seasonal availability of these foods can fluctuate. It is also because the dashed lines give the appearance of more than one season associated with each food type, thereby possibly overrepresenting the actual number of seasons of site use.

Identified species of charred nutshell and seed remains recovered from flotation samples of the four analyzed features (2, 15, 16, and 22) and from field screens at Feature 13 suggest seasons of occupation ranging from late spring through fall (Largy 1994). Limitations exist, however, in interpreting seasonality of occupation from plant remains. For example, both acorns and hickory nuts ripen in the fall, but their presence in the above five features at Lambert Farm does not necessarily mean that they were eaten during the fall. Nuts may have been stored for consumption during the lean winter months when Native American food supplies were usually low. Charred seeds and/or seed fragments (39 total) were recovered from Features 2, 16, and 22. According to Largy (1994), the carbonized seeds identified in Feature 2 became available in late spring through late summer. The identified charred seeds from Feature 16 suggest mid- to late summer availability. Feature 22 contained identified carbonized seeds available from midsummer into fall. Future analysis of flotation samples that were not examined by Largy, as well as the unanalyzed 236 nutshell and seed remains recovered in field screens, may provide additional seasonality estimates for Lambert Farm.

Lambert Farm is not the only prehistoric site in the Northeast that contained coastal resources suggesting more than one season of occupation. The Greenwich Cove site, located on Potowomut Neck approximately 3.1 miles (5 km) southeast of Lambert Farm (see Figure 1.2), was occupied relatively year-round for at least the last 2,000 years of prehistory (Bernstein 1993). Also on Potowomut Neck, near the Greenwich Cove site, quahog and deer remains, which I excavated in three separate Woodland shell middens, represented a summer–early fall seasonality (Kerber 1984, 1985). Farther to the east at archaeological sites on Cape Cod, Hancock's (1984) analysis of quahog growth patterns identified primarily winter and early-spring seasons of death. Similarly, from the lower Merrimack Valley in northeastern Massachusetts, Barber (1983) reconstructed multiple seasonality based on growth patterns of shellfish and other animal remains from six prehistoric sites. To the south, evidence from growth patterns of quahog and softshell clams recovered on eastern Long Island indicated year-round seasons of harvest (Lightfoot and Cerrato 1988, 1989). In addition to these similarities with other sites in the region, Lambert Farm contained some remarkable discoveries, including the three dog burials, which are discussed in the next chapter.

CHAPTER 4
Discoveries

The vast majority of archaeological remains from Lambert Farm, as is typical for prehistoric sites, consisted of stone chipping debris. There were also, of course, the usual types of stone artifacts, such as projectile points, knives, drills, and scrapers, as well as pottery sherds and abundant animal and plant remains, as discussed in the previous chapter. In addition to these objects were some rare discoveries. This chapter details the unusual finds and features. Included here are descriptions, analyses, and interpretations of the three dog burials.

UNUSUAL FINDS

Among the rare items found at Lambert Farm were several stone tools discovered together in an unusual association directly beside (but apparently separate from) Feature 22, the third dog burial. They were retrieved during our Phase Two excavation of the feature, between 30 and 40 cm (about 12–16 in) below ground surface in EU 64 but were not contained within the feature. These artifacts were a flake tool made of quartzite; two hammerstones made of cumberlandite and used to make chipped-stone artifacts; two graphite objects, possibly used for paint; a peculiar sandstone object that was ground into the shape of a top and perhaps used as a gaming stone; and two beautiful groundstone grooved axes. The latter three artifacts are illustrated in Figure 4.1. While these unusual eight items were not intrusive into Feature 22, their connection with the dog burial, if any, is unknown.

Some of the fascinating discoveries of organic remains at Lambert Farm, excluding the dog burials, consisted of bones and teeth. Various bone artifacts were found, including a serrated tool; a bead cut from bird bone; matching halves of a perforated object, perhaps a sewing needle; and a possible awl used for piercing hides (Figure 4.2). All of these bone tools were recovered from shell features, accounting for their exceptional preservation. Three other bones, all white-tailed deer phalanges (toe bones), were longitudinally perforated, perhaps done for use in the "pin and cup" game as played by Native Americans in the early historic period or even as decorative items (George 1993). These bone artifacts also were preserved within three shell deposits, including Feature 2.

While the vast majority of teeth unearthed at Lambert Farm were of white-tailed deer, three shark teeth (and shark vertebrae) and two human teeth were found. Shark remains are not well represented at northeastern sites, possibly due to the difficulty

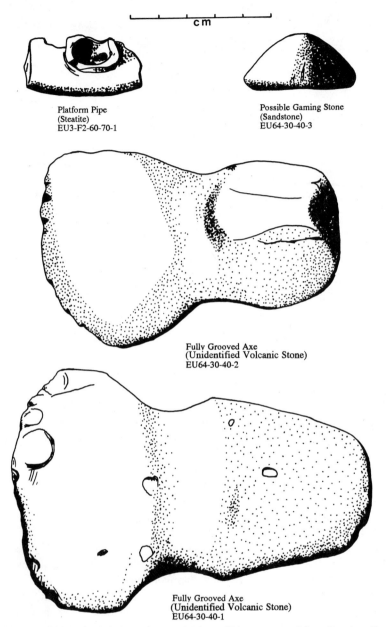

Platform Pipe
(Steatite)
EU3-F2-60-70-1

Possible Gaming Stone
(Sandstone)
EU64-30-40-3

Fully Grooved Axe
(Unidentified Volcanic Stone)
EU64-30-40-2

Fully Grooved Axe
(Unidentified Volcanic Stone)
EU64-30-40-1

FIGURE 4.1   Illustration of unusual groundstone artifacts recovered from Lambert Farm.

of catching sharks and the poor preservation quality of these remains. The shark teeth from Lambert Farm were uncovered in three shell deposits amd were identified as belonging to Sand Tiger Shark *(Odontaspis taurus)* (Handley 1996:28). Though it is conceivable that the Lambert Farm residents scavenged beached sharks, it is more likely that they hunted these animals offshore, since sharks tend to sink

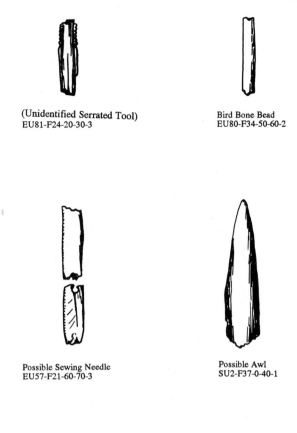

(Unidentified Serrated Tool)
EU81-F24-20-30-3

Bird Bone Bead
EU80-F34-50-60-2

Possible Sewing Needle
EU57-F21-60-70-3

Possible Awl
SU2-F37-0-40-1

cm

FIGURE 4.2   Illustration of selected bone artifacts recovered from Lambert Farm.

upon death (Handley 1996:31). The two human teeth were found in separate sample units. Both were deciduous, so-called "baby teeth." Thus, they likely represented natural losses, as opposed to burials, since no other human skeletal remains were identified at the site; nevertheless, the possibility exists that human burials occurred at Lambert Farm but were not detected by our sampling. Finally, we recovered a few large beaver incisors which appeared worn from use as tools, perhaps for incising and abrading.

SHELL FEATURES

A total of 49 features, all found below ground, were recorded at Lambert Farm. Every feature contained some amount of shells, ranging from small, thin scatters measuring a few centimeters in thickness to extraordinarily dense accumulations, some measuring 65 cm in thickness and 1 m in diameter (i.e., Features 2 and 22), which are discussed in the next section. Several deposits consisted entirely of one or two shellfish species, while others, namely Features 2 and 22, had as many as seven. By far most of the features at Lambert Farm were shell midden refuse or storage pits, representing the remains of consumed or planned meals.

Two features, however, were quite different from the rest, not because they yielded animal burials but because they contained postmolds. A postmold is a feature that consists of a soil discoloration indicating a hole in which a post once stood before it decayed. They are usually detected either in profile or on the floor of a sample unit. Postmolds are the primary evidence of wooden structures built by prehistoric Native Americans in the Northeast. In each of the two features, Feature 3 in STP T05-42.5 and Feature 24 in EU 81, a single postmold was recorded in one of the walls of the respective sample unit. Both postmolds were similar in that they appeared at about 10 cm below ground surface and extended to about 50 cm below ground surface. In addition, both ranged in width from 8 cm (about 3 in) at the top to 4 cm (about 1.5 in) at the bottom, giving them a tapered appearance. The purpose of the original posts is unknown. They may have served as supports for a shelter or even for a drying rack on which meat may have been smoked over a fire.

In two other features the remains of animal skeletons, this time not dogs, were found. One consisted of articulated bones of a possible raccoon. They were never identified by a specialist, since the animal did not appear to be associated with the prehistoric settlement of Lambert Farm. It probably died of natural causes within the past 50 years or so, as the well-preserved bones were encountered close to the surface. The other feature was a portion of a carcass of a large bird, most likely turkey. Once again, the bones were not analyzed, since we suspected that they dated no older than the historic use of the site; they could even have been the remains of a recent Thanksgiving dinner by the Lambert family. Many other historic materials, from the eighteenth to the early twentieth centuries, were found within the investigated 1.8 acres. These included rusty nails, broken pieces of glass and ceramics, smoking pipes made of white clay from England called kaolin, and ironically, an Indian-head penny. Unearthing historic artifacts from the site, however, came as no surprise. Lambert Farm obviously continued to be used long after it was abandoned by prehistoric Native Americans.

THE DOG BURIALS

Dog burials were discovered in Features 2 and 22. Feature 2 was first identified about 25 cm below ground surface in STP T01-50 during the first session of the 1988 field school. At the time, it appeared to be a rather nondescript shell midden as we removed a thick concentration of shells from the STP, along with fragments of animal bones and some chipping debris and charcoal. On the completion of the unit, we decided to expand our excavation of the feature by placing EU 3, a 1 × 1-m square, directly along the STP's west wall where the shell deposit was most dense. Sure enough, at about 25 cm deep in EU 3 we began to come across a thick concentration of shells, especially in the southern portion of the excavation unit, arranged in a semicircular manner.

As we continued removing the feature and its matrix in 5-cm levels, we noted three unusual patterns in the distribution of the shells. First, the deeper we excavated the more shells we uncovered, so that by about 50 cm below ground surface the floors of the levels were entirely covered by tightly compacted shells. This pattern is consistent with the shape of a mound—minimum exposure at the top, maximum exposure at the bottom. Second, the feature contained the remains of practically every shellfish species present in nearby Narragansett Bay, specifically, quahog, softshell clam, oyster, bay scallop, knobbed whelk, razor clam, and ribbed mussel. Even more fascinating, the densities of these individual species fluctuated among levels. Though precise measurements were not taken due to time and budgetary constraints, scallop shells, for instance, were situated predominantly toward the bottom of the feature and quahog shells toward the top. Third, many of the shells were complete, including several that were never opened. Most shell middens in the Northeast, however, tend to contain many more broken pieces of shells, probably caused by removing the shellfish meat.

We also were struck by the sheer wealth of material removed from the feature. Besides the countless shells, the feature contained several large, burned rocks; charcoal; pottery sherds; and an enormous amount of well-preserved but fragmented bones and teeth, mostly the remains of white-tailed deer and some wild turkey, sturgeon, muskrat, and moose. In addition, a few surprises were found among these objects. The first was chipping debris made of nonlocal raw materials, namely jasper from Pennsylvania and chert from New York. Next were mica fragments and a quartz crystal, items not commonly found at prehistoric sites in the region. Also, to our amazement and delight, we recovered a nearly complete platform smoking pipe carved out of steatite, also called soapstone (Figure 4.1). Little did we know that even more unusual finds were buried in this complex feature.

At about 90 cm (nearly 3 ft) below ground surface, the shells finally stopped appearing, marking what presumably was the bottom of the shell mound but, as we soon realized, not the bottom of the feature. Curiously, at this level was a large stone slab covering much of the southern portion of the excavation unit. By this time the entire field school crew had assembled in silence around EU 3 and, like me, probably asked themselves, "What could possibly be buried beneath this flat rock?" Given the importance of this feature, I took over the digging at this point. With all eyes fixed on my trowel, I carefully removed the stone slab. Using a soft brush to clear the soil below, I began to expose the fragmented remains of what looked like a very young animal. The bones appeared to have been crushed, possibly from the weight of the overlying slab and shell mound, but also perhaps from the cause of the animal's death; we would have to wait for future analysis to shed light on this issue. Though many bones were broken, others were still articulated. I knew the animal was not human, and, judging from the jaw and the intact deciduous teeth, popularly called milk teeth, I suspected a puppy; this was later confirmed by a specialist at PAL.

As I revealed more of the articulated skeleton, it became clear that this was a burial and not the remains of a meal that was subsequently discarded. The dog was laid to rest in an extended position, stretched out, lying on its right side with its head pointing northeast and its face toward west. Someone had even placed in the grave two shells, a knobbed whelk and a valve of softshell clam, the only shells found under the stone slab. Why was this dog, perhaps a pet of a Native American child, so carefully buried here and then covered by a large rock and a mound of shells? This question and others are addressed shortly. After the bones were removed, I continued to excavate the unit until quickly reaching sterile, glacial subsoil immediately below the burial at a depth of 100 cm. After four long days, EU 3 finally had been completed, but part of the feature still remained, as made abundantly clear by the 65-cm (about 2-ft) wall of shells and other debris imbedded in the south profile of the excavation unit. Unfortunately, we would have to wait a few weeks, which seemed like the proverbial eternity, for the Phase One operation to begin removing what was left of Feature 2.

The Phase One crew consisted of five PAL archaeologists, including myself, who had a maximum of two weeks to finish the excavation of the feature before it would be destroyed by construction of Spinnaker Lane (Figure 4.3). We worked quickly, despite the occurrence of a heat wave that set records across the Northeast in mid-July 1988. We set up three contiguous 1 × 1-m EUs surrounding the feature: EU 6 adjacent to the west wall of the previously completed EU 3; EU 7 adjacent to the south wall of EU 6; and EU 8 adjacent to the south wall of EU 3, where most of the remaining feature was expected. Thus, the total area excavated around and including Feature 2 was 2 × 2 m (about 6.5 × 6.5 ft). The three adjoining EUs were excavated simultaneously in 5-cm levels to obtain maximum horizontal exposure of the feature. Just as in EU 3, densely concentrated shells began to appear, primarily in EU 8, at about 25 cm deep. They were arranged in a semicircular pattern in the

FIGURE 4.3   PAL archaeologists excavating Feature 2 and the second dog burial during Phase One. The author is at the far left.

northern portion of EU 8, completing the full circular shape of the shell deposit as projected from the part of the feature previously exposed at 25 cm in EU 3. The contents of the feature were similar to those found in the portion excavated in EU 3, except that no smoking pipes, mica fragments, or quartz crystals were retrieved.

If there were other burials, dog or even human, in this feature, we expected them below 90 cm at the bottom of the shell mound. Once again we were surprised. Midway between the 70–75-cm (about 2.3–2.5-ft) level in EU 8, at a depth of 73 cm below ground surface, we encountered the skeletal remains of a second dog. Just like the first dog, this one was quite young, and many of its bones were broken but still articulated. After removing the surrounding soil and cultural debris, it was immediately obvious that this was a burial, separate from the other in EU 3. The dog was laid to rest in an extended position lying on its left side with its head pointing southeast and its face toward south. In contrast to the dog in EU 3, this second dog was buried on top of a stone slab placed within the same shell mound. Figure 4.4 schematically illustrates the position of the two burials and the shell deposit at different levels in EUs 3 and 8; the fragmentary condition of the skeletal remains of both dogs prevented a more detailed drawing. Mandible and maxilla fragments of the two dogs are photographed in Figure 4.5. Excavation of Feature 2 continued, without encountering any more burials. The dense concentration of shells remained in the feature (mostly in EU 8) until about 90 cm deep. At 100 cm deep it was over— sterile, glacial subsoil was reached, as the crew sighed together in relief and exhaustion. Of the dozens of shell deposits I have excavated from Nantucket to Block Island over more than 15 years, I had never seen one quite as remarkable as this, at least until the following year!

This was not the last dog burial to be unearthed at Lambert Farm. Another extremely thick accumulation of shells, Feature 22, was discovered during the first session of the 1989 field school, almost exactly one year from the day Feature 2 was found. In nearly an identical situation, Feature 22 was first identified at about 25 cm below ground surface in STP T35-90, some 65 m (about 213 ft) northeast of Feature 2. As we removed more and more shells from the STP, I remember thinking nervously that I had seen this before. Indeed, as we were about to find out, it was all too familiar!

After completing the STP and finding primarily shell midden debris, I set up an adjoining 1 × 1-m square, designated EU 55, along the STP's west wall. There was no logical reason to select this direction for the EU, as shells were consistently dense in all four walls of the STP. I suppose it was just a hunch and, looking back, a lucky one. As EU 55 was excavated in 5-cm levels, thickly compacted shells entirely covered each level between about 25 and 85 cm (about 10–33 in) deep. There was no need to separate the feature from the matrix, since there essentially was no matrix in these levels, which contained very little beyond massive amounts of shells. Although most of the shells were quahogs and oysters, of which many were unbroken, Feature 22 yielded the same shellfish species as those in Feature 2, except for knobbed whelk. At about 85 cm deep in EU 55, the skull of an animal was uncovered. Clearly not human, it appeared rather to be yet another dog, much older than the previous two (Figures 4.6, page 71 and 4.7, page 72). The cranium and both mandibles are

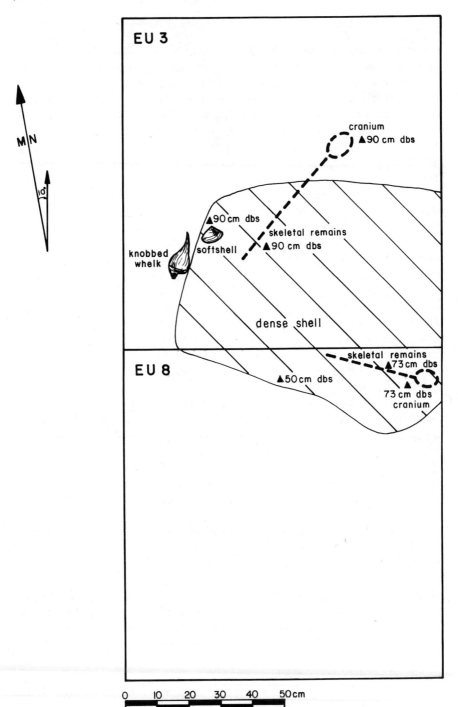

FIGURE 4.4   Plan view of two dog burials and other remains recovered from Feature 2, EUs 3 and 8, at Lambert Farm (from Kerber et al. 1989:170).

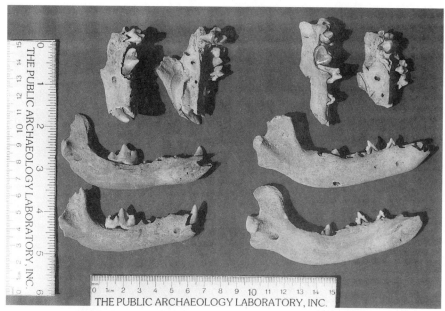

FIGURE 4.5   Mandible (bottom) and maxilla (top) fragments of the two dogs excavated in
Feature 2, EU 3 (right) and EU 8 (left).

FIGURE 4.6   Portion of dog burial discovered in Feature 22, EU 55 at 90 cm below
ground surface. Shell mound below which the dog was interred can be seen in the western
and northern side walls of EU 55 (arrow points north).

FIGURE 4.7   Close-up of dog burial in Feature 22, EU 55.

illustrated in Figure 4.8. To the disappointment of the field school participants, however, we were forced to backfill the excavation unit, since there was no time remaining in the session to expose and remove the entire burial. We returned a little more
than a month later with a group of volunteers to take up where we had left off.

During this Phase Two period, in which we worked on both days of a mid-July
weekend in 1989, most of the feature was excavated. We began by digging out the
filled-in portion of EU 55. Next, just like at Feature 2, we placed three contiguous
1 × 1-m EUs surrounding Feature 22: EU 62 adjacent to the west wall of EU 55, where
most of the remaining feature was expected; EU 63 adjacent to the north wall of
EU 62; and EU 64 adjacent to the north wall of EU 55 (Figure 4.9). Similarly, the
total area excavated around and including Feature 22 was 2 × 2 m. The three adjoining EUs were dug simultaneously in 5-cm levels as done at Feature 2. A thick concentration of shells appeared at about 25 cm and was mostly confined to a small
portion along the eastern edge of EU 62. The deeper levels of EU 62 contained increasingly more shells, eventually distributed horizontally across most of the unit.
This pattern, as was also seen in Feature 2, indicated the shape of a mound which
happened to be centered between EUs 55 and 62. In addition to the thousands upon

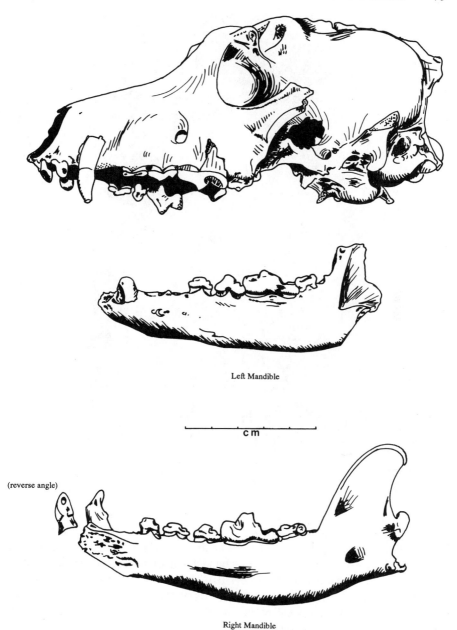

Left Mandible

c m

(reverse angle)

Right Mandible

FIGURE 4.8   Illustration of dog cranium and mandibles recovered from Feature 22 at Lambert Farm.

thousands of shells, the feature held remains of charcoal, pottery sherds, chipping debris (all local raw materials), and many well-preserved but frequently broken bones and teeth, mostly of white-tailed deer, some tautog (fish), and possibly wild turkey.

When we reached the bottom of the shell mound at 85–90 cm below ground surface in EUs 55 and 62, the skeleton of the entire dog was visible. The bones were

FIGURE 4.9   PAL archaeologists excavating Feature 22 and the third dog burial during Phase Two. Alan Leveillee is in the foreground, and author is at the far left.

nearly all intact and in excellent condition, unlike the burials in Feature 2. Surrounding the dog's skull were several complete softshell clams, perhaps left by the owner as grave offerings. The dog was placed in a flexed position, curled up, lying on its left side with its front left paw carefully tucked under its head, which was pointing east and its face toward south (Figure 4.10). The precise position of the burial remains was mapped (Figure 4.11). After removing the ribs, we discovered that the lumbar vertebrae, popularly called the lower backbone, were in a contorted, unnatural arrangement as if the body were intentionally folded to fit into a small burial pit (Figure 4.12). These bones in particular were delicately taken out of the ground since they also could provide evidence of the animal's cause of death, to be studied later in the lab. As time ran out of the Phase Two operation, we would have to wait a few more weeks for the start of the second session of the 1989 field school to resume the burial excavation. No more surprises were encountered on completion of this feature, which was not the case for its subsequent analysis, as you will see next.

FIGURE 4.10   Dog burial exposed in Feature 22, EUs 55 and 62, at 90 cm below ground surface. The dog is in a flexed position, lying on its left side with its front left paw tucked under its head. Note the several softshell clams next to the skull.

FIGURE 4.11   PAL archaeologists Ruth Greenspan (foreground) and Mary Lynn Rainey mapping dog burial in Feature 22, EUs 55 and 62, at 90 cm below ground surface.

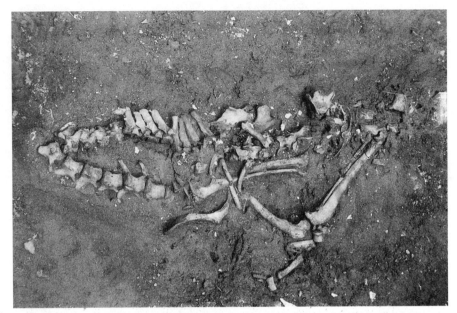

FIGURE 4.12   Vertebrae and other bones of dog burial in Feature 22, EUs 55 and 62, at 90 cm below ground surface. Note the contorted, unnatural position of the lumbar vertebrae at the left.

The skeletal remains of the three dogs recovered from Lambert Farm were analyzed in two separate studies by Greenspan (Greenspan 1993; Kerber et al. 1989). The objective was to evaluate the completeness and condition of the bones and to identify the level of maturity, presence of disease (if any), and cause(s) of death for each individual. The results of Greenspan's analysis are summarized here and contribute to investigating the occurrence of prehistoric canine mortuary ceremonialism at the site.

Analysis of the articulated skeletal remains from Feature 2 indicates that both dogs were approximately five to six months old based on the sequence of tooth eruption (Miller et al. 1964:652–53). Although one of the individuals was slightly larger than the other, it was not possible to determine sex for either dog. Also, no clues as to possible cause of death were evident, and no cut marks were found on any of the bones. Similarly, Greenspan was unable to identify any evidence as to cause of death of the dog buried in Feature 22. The age of this dog was determined to be five or six years old and was a male, as identified by the baculum (penis bone).

During her analysis of the dog burial in Feature 22, Greenspan made a startling discovery. She identified in the 80–90-cm level below ground surface in the feature an extra left distal portion of a humerus, or front upper leg bone, from a juvenile dog. The bone was cut from the humerus of a dog that was not the one buried in Feature 22, as cut marks were clearly visible on the piece. Coincidentally, the burial of the juvenile dog in EU 8 Feature 2 was missing a left distal portion of a humerus (Kerber et al. 1989:168). Greenspan (1993) suspected in her report (prior to comparison of the two bone specimens) that the fragment from Feature 22 might be from the juvenile dog buried in EU 8 Feature 2. Such speculation is even more conceivable when the calibrated radiocarbon dates from the two burials are compared. Indeed, the two dogs may have died in the same year, sometime between 790–660 B.P., the overlap between the two dates (Table 3.1); this presumes that the age of the shell radiocarbon sample in EU 3 Feature 2 is the same age as the juvenile dog from EU 8 buried in the feature. But much to our disappointment, the two humerus portions did not fit together—they were not part of the same bone. The Feature 22 specimen is from a significantly more mature (though not full-grown) dog than the one in EU 8 Feature 2 (Greenspan, personal communication 1993).

Why was this odd bone cut from a young dog's leg and then placed in the burial of an older dog? Was this bone from a consumed meal, part of a sacrifice placed in the adult male dog burial, or both? Presumably, it is different from the disarticulated canid bone remains analyzed by George that were recovered in Feature 22. Those specimens were situated in levels above the dog burial and are from adult canid(s). These and several other perplexing questions concerning Features 2 and 22 and their associated dog burials are still unanswered. Obviously, a great amount of effort and care was taken in the preparation and placement of the three dog burials and in the construction of the two shell mounds, especially in light of the site's one-mile distance from Narragansett Bay. The question remains why? Although there is no physical evidence on the skeletal remains indicating that the three dogs were sacrificed, were their deaths part of a religious ceremony marking an important event in the society? Are the abundant remains of animal and plant food in both shell mounds and the smoking pipe in Feature 2 evidence of a ritual feast associated with the dog burials? Also, did the shells in Features 2 and 22 possess religious/ideological meaning in contrast to the common archaeological interpretation of these remains as "midden refuse?" While we may never know the answers to these questions, there is ample room for conjecture.

First, of all the shell deposits discovered at Lambert Farm, Features 2 and 22 contained the densest concentrations of mollusc remains at the site. It may be no coincidence that these two features also held dog burials. While some of the shellfish remains in both features may represent food refuse, perhaps even in connection with ritual feasting associated with the burying of dogs, it is conceivable that many of the shells possessed symbolic importance as raw materials for the two burial mounds. Testing such a hypothesis would be difficult. Nevertheless, the possibility of an ideological function of shell is an intriguing one. Archaeologists typically separate spirituality and ceremonialism from subsistence, though such a division was probably far less rigid among Native Americans. Thus, in some cases prehistoric shell fishing might have been as centrally related to spirituality and ceremonialism as it was to subsistence. For many Native Americans shell fishing was likely more than just an easy way to obtain a meal. Indeed, the Lambert Farm data emphasize the danger in assuming that all dense shell deposits were simply "midden refuse." Claassen (1991) even proposed an ideological value of freshwater shells and shell fishing for the Shell Mound Archaic period in the Southeast and Midwest regions of the United States. In addition, Blukis Onat (1985) interpreted shells as not just garbage but as raw material for community engineering among Native Americans from the Northwest Coast region of the United States and southern Canada.

The seasonality of the analyzed shell samples from Features 2 and 22 provide ammunition for additional speculation. Both features contained quahog shells that were gathered during all four seasons of the year. Thus, analyzed quahog shells may not have been deposited in each of these two features during one season in conjunction with a separate or the same ceremonial event, as otherwise may have been reasonably assumed. Rather, these shells, collected from Narragansett Bay, were presumably brought to the site over several seasons following the initial burying of the associated dogs. It is also possible, however, that the seasons of death of the analyzed quahog shell specimens are not necessarily the same as the seasons in which the dog burial features were constructed. In such a scenario, for instance, both features could contain quahog shells that were removed from Narragansett Bay during four different seasons, carried to Lambert Farm for consumption of shellfish meat, and discarded in deposits older than Features 2 and 22. Months or even years later these shells were removed (i.e., "mined") from their original deposits at the site and redeposited (i.e., "recycled") in both features in association with a separate or the same ceremonial event.

In effect, if shells (at least quahog) were considered an ideologically important raw material with which to construct the two dog burial mounds, perhaps shells "mined" from older features previously left at Lambert Farm would provide the same purpose as shells collected from Narragansett Bay and directly placed in Features 2 and 22. If the mined quahog shells were previously gathered from the bay during different seasons, evidence of this would presumably be detected by the seasonality analysis of the specimens in Features 2 and 22, even though these same shells could have been redeposited in each burial mound during one season in connection with a ceremony. Unfortunately, testing such a hypothesis is not possible, at least at present. It would depend, in part, on precise age determinations, currently not available by radiocarbon dating, of quahog shell and articulated canine bone from both features. Perhaps with future development of more accurate dating techniques we might some day be able to pursue this stimulating hypothesis.

So the question remains—why were the Lambert Farm dog burials given such elaborate treatment? Were these dogs more than just pets to the prehistoric residents of the site? We turn now to Chapter 5, which examines the role of dogs in Native American life and death. This subject is presented within a larger context, drawing on comparative archaeological and ethnohistorical material from the Northeast and other regions. Such a broad perspective provides insight into the topic of Native American treatment of dogs in general and the meaning of the dog remains at Lambert Farm in particular.

CHAPTER 5

Native American Treatment of Dogs: Lambert Farm in Global Perspective

Archaeologists tend to rely on a comparative approach in trying to develop hypotheses by which to judge their data. In this chapter the topic of Native American treatment of dogs is placed within a broader context by discussing archaeological and ethnohistorical information from northeastern North America and elsewhere. This material allows us to compare Lambert Farm with other prehistoric dog burial sites and also sheds light on the various roles dogs played in Native American societies. Before presenting the archaeological and ethnohistorical data, it is helpful to provide a brief overview of the origins of dogs.

ANCESTRY OF DOGS

The remains of dogs around the world have generated considerable interest, perhaps more than those of other domesticated animals. As stated by Stanley Olsen (1979:188; 1985:xi), this may be due to both the unusual place we have given the dog in our own culture and our long and favorable relationship with this social animal. The origins of dogs have long been the subject of research among many archaeologists and zoologists. Much of it, however, is beyond the scope of this book and can only be briefly summarized here.

But first, in order to begin to understand this complex history, we need to consider the larger group of which all dogs are a part—canids or members of the family Canidae. In addition to dogs, canids consist of wolves, coyotes, jackals, and foxes. Today there are some 36 species of canids within 12 genera, depending on which of the many classifications one uses (McLoughlin 1983:ix). There has only been one species of dog *(Canis familiaris),* however. In addition, eight living species of wolves, jackals, and coyotes are the other members of the genus *Canis* (McLoughlin 1983:69,146); foxes belong to the genus *Vulpes.* Although not common, all nine of the *Canis* species can interbreed to produce fertile hybrid offspring (McLoughlin 1983:69). Of the 36 species of canids, dogs are the only one that was domesticated. In fact, they were the first animal in the world to be domesticated and the only animal domesticated by Native North Americans, except for the turkey in the southwestern United States. If it were not for human intervention through selective breeding, dogs would never have come into existence; there is no such thing as a nondomesticated dog, though wild or feral dogs still exist today. Dogs also enjoy the widest range and greatest numbers of all canids. At present there are more than

400 distinct breeds of dog around the globe (all members of the same species) and over 80 million dogs in the United States alone (Clutton-Brock 1987:34; McLoughlin 1983:83). With the rat, mouse, and domesticated cat, the dog is one of the few mammals that have lived in every part of the world settled by people (McLoughlin 1983:ix).

Much has been written on the origins of dogs. One of the earliest papers on the subject was written in 1787 by Hunter, who presented evidence to argue that the dog, wolf, and jackal were all the same species. In 1803 the origins of the American dog were discussed by Barton. He wrote that many historians and naturalists in his day asserted that there were no dogs in the Americas prior to European colonization. The prevailing view at the time was that Native American dogs resulted from breeding European-introduced dogs with wolves and other canids in the Western Hemisphere (Barton 1803:1). Studies of the different dog breeds were published by at least the mid–nineteenth century (e.g., Smith 1839), and in 1868 Darwin offered his views on the origins of dogs.

It was not until the twentieth century that the first extensive study of North American dogs was produced by Allen (1920). In his lengthy monograph, Allen (1920:503) concluded from descriptions in travelers' reports and remains from archaeological sites that there were three general sizes of aboriginal dogs in North America: a large, broad-muzzled Eskimo dog and a larger and smaller form of "Indian dog," both of which were believed to comprise 16 varieties. This publication is now out of date, as many later studies and critical finds have refuted much of Allen's classification scheme. The next comprehensive review was completed by Haag (1948), who analyzed the remains of prehistoric dogs from widespread areas of North America. Haag's work, which is also out of date, was similar to Allen's as it divided aboriginal North American dogs into three general size groups. From his sample, Haag (1948:258) detected that the smaller dogs dated to older periods than the larger ones.

Today, the development of prehistoric dogs in North America and elsewhere continues to be studied. Much data have been gathered since the earlier writings, but the picture is far from complete. The beginnings of canid ancestry are poorly understood due to a lack of evidence. The earliest fossil carnivores that are believed to be related to canids are miacids, animals with long, extended tails that lived about 40 million years ago and varied in size between a modern-day fox and a ferret (S.Olsen 1985:2,3). By about 15 million years ago ancient canids had extended their range to the Eastern Hemisphere, making them the only animals, except for the camel and the horse, that originated in North America and eventually migrated to other continents (S.Olsen 1985:3). Millions of years later, by at least 12,000 B.P. (ca. 10,000 B.C.), domestication of dogs occurred independently among hunters and gatherers in several widely separated places in the world (Olsen and Olsen 1977:533).

Specialists agree that the domesticated dog evolved from a small subspecies of wolf in a number of parallel and partly separate regional occurrences of domestication (S.Olsen 1985; Morey 1992, cited in Wapnish and Hesse 1993:76–77). It is impossible to say, however, whether humans or wolves initiated the process of domestication. Stanley Olsen (1985:16) believed that wolves were predisposed to taming and ultimately to domestication by humans because of their mutually compatible social organizations. This is partly why dogs were the first domesticated animal, as stated by Olsen (1979:192):

> ... of all the domestic animals having early origins, only the dog would fit into the social patterns of a human hunter-gatherer society. Those that followed would more naturally be associated with the beginnings of agriculture and a sedentary way of life.

The domestication of dogs may have followed the taming of wolves, but these two processes are quite different. Taming involves keeping a nondomesticated animal as a pet or food source and may occur with almost any wild creature. It might take several weeks or more for the animal to be tamed. Domestication, on the other hand, takes place over many generations through selective breeding controlled by humans that may result in the appearance of a new species. The process of domestication of dogs has led to changes in their behavior and appearance over hundreds and thousands of years and, together with the work of dog breeders in the past several centuries, has resulted in the enormous variety of dogs that we see in the world today. Among the first observable physical changes are the foreshortening of the muzzle, or rostrum, and the facial area, crowding of tooth rows, and overall reduction in tooth size (S.Olsen 1985:19).

We do not know when and where dogs were first domesticated. Part of the problem in determining this is due to the difficulty in knowing whether the often fragmentary bones found belong to dogs or to wild species of the same genus; complete skeletons are virtually unknown. Theories of the origins of domesticated dogs have focused on the Near East and western Europe where some of the oldest specimens have been found with the remains of prehistoric hunters and gatherers. But, as you will also see, other researchers have looked to China for a separate center of dog domestication.

The most commonly cited remains of the oldest domesticated dog in the world are a few teeth and a left mandible portion (Figure 5.1) recovered 2 feet below the floor of Palegawra Cave in northeastern Iraq (see Figure 5.2) by Braidwood and Howe between 1945 and 1955 (Olsen 1979:191). The significance of these finds was not known until many years later when Turnbull and Reed (1974) reanalyzed and identified the specimens as belonging to domesticated dog. A sample submitted for fluorine analysis conducted by the British Museum of Natural History dated to

FIGURE 5.1   Canid mandible portion from Palegawra Cave, Iraq (from S. Olsen 1985:75).

Legend

1 Palegawra Cave	11 Ashkelon
2 Star Carr	12 Yin
3 Zhoukoudian	13 Rodgers Shelter
4 Pan-p'o	14 Koster
5 Jaguar Cave	15 White Dog Cave
6 Agate Basin	16 Ventana Cave
7 Fairbanks Creek	17 Eva
8 Grasshopper Pueblo	18 Indian Knoll
9 Ein Mallaha	19 Keatley Creek
10 Abydos	20 Paloma

FIGURE 5.2   World map, showing site locations outside northeastern North America mentioned in the text.

about 14,000 B.P. (ca. 12,000 B.C.) (Flanagan 1975:54). But Stanley Olsen (1985:72–73) claimed that the specimens are not clearly from a domesticated dog as they also exhibit some wolf characteristics. He (S.Olsen 1985:xii,71) also questioned most of the very early fragmentary remains of other so-called dogs, including the bones of a small young dog from Star Carr in Yorkshire, England, radiocarbon dated to 7538 ± 350 B.C. (ca. 9500 B.P.) (Degerbøl 1961, cited in S.Olsen 1985:71). Evidence of early canids, many of which are presumed to be domesticated, also have been found in several other countries in Europe, Asia, and North and South America, including Israel, Denmark, Russia, Turkey, Japan, China, the United States, and Peru.

The ancestor of early North American dogs is believed by many to be a particularly small subspecies of wolf, called the Chinese or Asian wolf *(Canis lupus chanco),* which originated in China and Mongolia (Lawrence 1967; S. Olsen 1985:41; Olsen and Olsen 1977:533). According to present consensus, dogs did not exist in North America until they were brought by the first human settlers to the continent. These people and presumably their dogs migrated from northeastern Asia, perhaps as early as 15,000 B.P. (ca. 13,000 B.C.), where dogs had been previously domesticated. For instance, at Zhoukoudian, southwest of Beijing in northern China, skeletal remains of a small wolf *(Canis lupus variabilis)* were found with stone tools, dating between 500,000 and 200,000 B.P., that were produced by hominids, or early human ancestors, known as *Homo erectus pekinensis* (S. Olsen 1985:15, 42, 44). Although this is one of the oldest known associations of wolves and hominids in the world, there is no evidence that these canids were tamed or domesticated by the early human ancestors. The earliest known remains of domesticated dog in China are dated to 4865 B.C. (almost 7000 B.P.) and come from Pan-p'o, an early Neolithic period site in Shensi Province (Olsen 1979:191).

Until recently, it was believed that the oldest known domesticated dog remains from North America were recovered in excavations from Jaguar Cave in Indian Head Canyon on the west slope of the Beaverhead Mountains in southeastern Idaho (Lawrence 1967:47). The specimens consisted of incomplete mandibles, a single left mandible, and a small portion of a left maxilla (lower skull fragment) that indicated the presence of two different-sized dogs (S.Olsen 1985:31; Pferd 1987:46); the smaller dog was similar in size to a present-day terrier, and the larger dog was about the size of a husky (Pferd 1987:9). Charcoal from a hearth in the same test unit and level as two paired mandibles was radiocarbon dated to 10,370 ± 350 B.P. (ca. 8400 B.C.) (Pferd 1987:45). We currently know, however, that these specimens are much younger. Recent AMS dates suggest that the age is no more than 3,000–4,000 B.P. (Gowlett et al. 1987:145–46; Clutton-Brock and Noe-Nygaard 1990:645, cited in Morey and Wiant 1992:225). It is now thought that the oldest well-documented dog remains from North America date to between 9,000 and 10,000 B.P. (7,000–8,000 B.C.) and were excavated at Danger Cave in Utah (Grayson 1988:23, cited in Morey and Wiant 1992:225). Prehistoric dog remains of similar antiquity have been found much farther south in the Andes Mountains of Peru, dating to about 11,000 B.P. (ca. 9000 B.C.) (Wing 1977).

Reports of other relatively early domesticated dog remains in North America are few and far between. Walker and Frison (1982:125) identified fragments of a skull and other bones of what they believed to be domesticated dog at the Agate Basin site in northeastern Wyoming. Although the specimens were not directly dated, their age was estimated at around 10,500–10,800 B.P. (ca. 8500–8800 B.C.), based on their recovery in the dated Paleoindian (Folsom culture) level. The size of the animal was relatively large, similar to that of prehistoric dogs whose remains had been uncovered at 11 other sites in Wyoming. In fact, Walker and Frison (1982:168) claimed that indigenous domesticated dogs that existed in Wyoming from Paleoindian to historic times were generally quite large, even bigger than the large individual from Jaguar Cave. The authors argued further that these large dogs represented crosses or hybrids between aboriginal North American large dogs and native wolves during the prehistoric period, thus causing their wolflike appearance (1982:165,168); it is unclear, however, whether this interbreeding was directed by Native Americans. Even ethnographers in the nineteenth century reported "large wolflike" dogs among Native Americans on the northwestern Plains (Figure 5.3), including the Missouri River area of Nebraska, North and South Dakota, and Montana (Walker and Frison 1982:128,165,167).

Wolves have a well-established record in North America, dating back to early Pleistocene times (S.Olsen 1985:12–13). Indeed, a skull of a wolf *(Canis lupus)* was collected at Fairbanks Creek in interior Alaska and dated by the AMS technique to 18,610 ± 165 B.P. (ca. 16,600 B.C.) (AA-3912), which corresponds to the peak of the last glaciation (Guthrie 1990:110). More recent remains have been found at other sites on the continent. In particular, the bones of an immature gray wolf were excavated at the Grasshopper Pueblo in Arizona, which dates to about 700–600 B.P.,

FIGURE 5.3   Assiniboin hunter and dogs from the northwestern Plains, photographed about 1906 by Edward S. Curtis. The Assiniboin are an offshoot of the Yanktonai Sioux, from whom they separated prior to 1640, and have long resided in the area encompassed by present-day Montana and Alberta (Cardozo 1993:82).

leading Stanley Olsen (1985:39–40) to speculate that the wolf pup may have been kept as a pet, perhaps even tamed (but not domesticated). No doubt domesticated dog-wolf interbreeding has a long history in parts of North America, especially on the Plains.

ARCHAEOLOGICAL EVIDENCE OF DOG BURIALS AND SACRIFICES AROUND THE WORLD

There are thousands of reported dog interments at archaeological sites across the globe, far too many to be included in this book. Instead, I provide brief summaries of some from several regions, including the Northeast, which is discussed at the end of this section. The information presented here, though it pertains to more than Native American cultures, helps to place the Lambert Farm dog burials within a larger context.

Some fascinating evidence of early mortuary treatment of dogs comes from Israel, Egypt, and China. One of the oldest known canine burials in the world was unearthed at Ein Mallaha (Eynan), an early Natufian period site in northern Israel. The remains are especially interesting in light of the Lambert Farm dog burials. In particular, the skeleton of a puppy, between three and five months old, was accompanied by the burial of an old woman (Davis 1987:147). This association was interpreted by Davis and Valla (1978:609–10) as indicative of an affectionate relationship with humans. The canid skeleton could not be identified definitively to species but was believed to be either a dog or wolf. Radiocarbon samples of the bone dated to 11,590 ± 540 B.P. (ca. 9600 B.C.) (LY 1660), 11,740 ± 570 B.P. (ca. 9700 B.C.) (LY 1661), and 11,310 ± 880 B.P. (ca. 9300 B.C.) (LY 1662; Davis and Valla 1978:610).

Among the world's largest number of dog burials are those discovered in ancient Egyptian villages, which often had cemeteries that contained mummified family dogs. For instance, at Abydos along the Nile River in Egypt, Peet (1914, cited in Wapnish and Hesse 1993:70) estimated that tens of thousands of mummified dogs were found, dating perhaps between 2100 and 1600 B.P. (ca. 100 B.C. and A.D. 350). Indeed, the Egyptian god Anubis, depicted as a human form with a dog's head, was believed to have supervised preparation of mummification rituals (Lurker 1974). Further, some of the oldest evidence in the world of dog burials placed in human graves is from Egypt, dating to around 8000 B.P. (ca. 6000 B.C.) (Haag 1948:253), which is consistent with the ancient Egyptian belief that the dog spirit served as guide to the land of the dead (Lurker 1974).

With the exception of Egyptian sites, the largest number of dog burials in the Mediterranean world were found at Ashkelon, a historic city port on the south coastal plain of Israel (Wapnish and Hesse 1993:67–68,75). More than 1,600 dog bones, representing possibly 600 to 700 dogs, were recently recovered in hundreds of burials, dating to an 80-year period between about 2500 and 2300 B.P. (ca. 500 and 300 B.C.; Hesse, personal communication 1994; Wapnish and Hesse 1993:57–59,74). The vast majority of the dogs were buried in fills above a large, previously used warehouse and in streets or thoroughfares between buildings. Several noteworthy observations were made by Wapnish and Hesse (1993:74) concerning the dog burials: The dogs died from a host of natural causes; there was no evidence of sacrifice; no interment was marked or accompanied by grave goods or human skeletal remains; many burials disturbed earlier graves; there was no evidence of cemeteries; each dog corpse was carefully placed in its grave; and no discernible pattern was in evidence in the orientation of the burial pits or in the placement of the dogs. The most striking characteristic of the dog burials, however, was the disproportionately larger number of puppies. Of the three identified age groups of dogs represented in the burials, puppies (0–6 months), subadults (6–18 months), and adults, puppies constituted 62% of the entire sample of dog skeletal remains (Wapnish and Hesse 1993:59–60). Based on the above evidence and other data, the authors (1993:74) concluded that the goal of burying the dogs at Ashkelon was not to produce a cemetery or preserve the memory of the animals. Instead, the dog burials at this Middle

Eastern urban center served more a practical purpose—to inter the carcasses—than a spiritual one. The act of burying dogs at Ashkelon presumably lacked the heightened ritual and religious significance prevalent at many other dog burial sites.

The importance of dogs among early Chinese populations is extraordinarily vivid during the Shang Dynasty, the first urbanized, bronze-using civilization of East Asia (J. Olsen 1985:60). One site in particular, called Yin, contained truly spectacular finds. Yin is located near Anyang in northern Henan Province and was an urban complex inhabited from about 1384 to 1100 B.C. (roughly 3300–3100 B.P.) (J. Olsen 1985:60). Between 1969 and 1977, 939 Shang tombs were excavated in the western portion of the site (Anyang Archaeological Team 1979, cited in J. Olsen 1985:60). While 17 tombs contained 38 human sacrifices, many others yielded the remains of sacrificed animals, mostly dogs; John Olsen (1985), however, did not provide specific evidence for the human and dog sacrifices. An astounding 439 sacrificial dogs were found in 339 excavated tombs (Anyang Archaeological Team 1979:46–48, cited in J. Olsen 1985:61). Many of the dogs were buried with bronze bells suspended from their necks, which further emphasized the importance of dogs as sacrifices, given the predominantly ceremonial use of bronze objects during this period (J. Olsen 1985:61).

In North America the number of recovered dog remains increases for the Archaic period. In addition, the oldest identified burials of dogs in the continent date to this time. The remainder of this section discusses some of the archaeological evidence of dog burials and sacrifices in North America, especially the Northeast.

At the Koster site, along the east bluff of the lower Illinois River in central Illinois, three dog skeletons were discovered in a canine cemetery in the eleventh cultural horizon of the site, dating to about 8500 B.P. (ca. 6500 B.C.) (Morey and Wiant; 1992:224; Struever and Holton 1979:47). These Early Archaic remains are the oldest known dog burials in North America and are among the oldest securely identified and dated domesticated dogs in the world (Morey and Wiant 1992:224,228). As Morey and Wiant (1992:225) explained, the three skeletons were recovered in small basin-shaped pits that were only large enough to accomodate the carcasses. Though each pit was no deeper than 15 cm, their association with Horizon 11 meant that they were situated 12–13 m below present ground surface. All three canids were buried lying on their sides. Figure 5.4 depicts a photograph of a burial containing one of the dog skeletons (specimen F-2357). In a different burial, the skull of a dog (specimen F-2256) was discovered near a metate and mano (food grinding tools), though it is unclear whether these artifacts were put in the grave (Morey and Wiant 1992:225). The three canids were about the same size. Two were male and one was presumably female (specimen F-2256). The articulated remains of the latter were associated with charcoal that was radiocarbon dated to 8470 ± 110 B.P. (ISGS-1762) (Morey and Wiant 1992:225). There were no signs of burning or cutting/skinning marks on the bones that might indicate that these dogs were eaten. Though the authors admitted the difficulty in reliably inferring the role of these dogs, they argued that the deliberate burial, combined with the absence of modification of the bones, not only suggested that the role was more than purely utilitarian. But this evidence also raised the possibility that an affectionate relationship existed between these

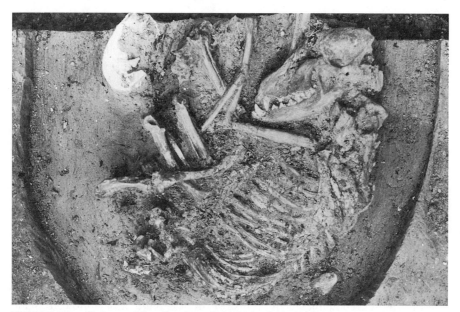

FIGURE 5.4   Skeleton of dog (Specimen F-2357) buried in Horizon 11 at Koster site, Illinois.

dogs and the prehistoric Native Americans at Koster over 8,000 years ago (Morey and Wiant 1992:228).

The remains of another dog were discovered at the Koster site. This burial contained the skeleton of a mature dog lying on its left side in a fire pit 29 feet below ground surface (Hill 1972:1, 3). The size of the dog was estimated to be about that of a fox terrier, slightly smaller than the small dog from Jaguar Cave (Hill 1972:3). Though Morey and Wiant (1992:225) claimed that this find was of problematical stratigraphic association and dating, Hill (1972:1) reported that two samples of charred wood associated with this burial were radiocarbon dated to 7000 ± 360 B.P. (ca. 5000 B.C.) and 7155 ± 220 B.P. (ca. 5100 B.C.) (Geochron). Nevertheless, what is especially remarkable about this burial is its striking similarity with three aspects of the more recent dog burials at Lambert Farm. First, the dog at the Koster site was buried in a "midden" that also contained the remains of at least 43 other animals, including freshwater shellfish (mussels), fish, turtle, deer, and many other mammals. Hill (1972:5) claimed that these remains appeared to be from refuse which was thrown into the fire pit along with soil to cover the dog. The metacarpals, or upper foot bones, of the left front foot were slightly singed from having been placed on the top of a fire in the fire pit. Hill (1972:5) concluded that the absence of other burned dog bones, in addition to the dog's position above the ashes in the pit, suggested that the dog was put in the pit when only a small fire remained. Second, in the thoracic region, or neck area, of the dog were found eight bone parts of an unidentified, small immature mammal, possibly a domesticated puppy. Third, the older dog's skull was crushed, which Hill (1972:1) presumed was due to the weight of the overlying soil rather than the cause of death. That none of the older dog's

bones was cut or broken purposely most likely indicated that the dog was not sacrificed or eaten but died of natural causes and was subsequently buried. Pferd (1987:48)
interpreted the Koster dog burial as part of a ritual. He believed that the dog's placement on top of a fire after death had religious significance. In his view, considerable
forethought and overt action were evident in the interment of this dog, which was so
valued that it received the same type of special care given to deceased persons (Pferd
1987:49).

Another well-known discovery of an early dog burial is from Rodgers Shelter,
located in the western Ozark highland of Missouri. McMillan (1970:1246) reported
that a small adult dog was buried in a prepared grave at this site. Charred wood from
the same level as the bones was radiocarbon dated to 5540 ± 170 B.C. (about 7500 B.P.)
(GAK-1172), making this one of the oldest known dog burials in the United States.
The skeletal remains of the dog, which was about the size of a fox terrier, were discovered during the summer of 1966 in a shallow pit beneath limestone rocks.
McMillan (1970:1246) reasoned that the position of the rocks were tilted down and
inward, suggesting a shallow basin-shaped pit prepared for interment.

Mummified dogs, exceedingly rare finds, were excavated in North America. At
White Dog Cave in northwestern Arizona, Guernsey and Kidder (1921) discovered
two well-preserved mummies of prehistoric dogs (Figure 5.5). Both were found
with several human mummies that were wrapped in fur robes, one of which contained dog hair (S.Olsen 1985:39). One dog was longhaired (buff color), about the
size of a small collie, with erect ears and a bushy tail. The other dog had a short-
haired, but shaggy, black-and-white coat, erect ears, and a long, bushy tail and was
considerably smaller, about the size of a terrier (S.Olsen 1985:35,39). The age of
both dogs is not precisely known, but they were associated with Basketmaker cultural ruins in the cave. Extrapolating from other known Basketmaker occurrences, it
is likely that the dogs date to between about 2200 and 1800 B.P. (ca. 200 B.C. and
A.D. 200) (John Olsen, personal communication 1995). At another site, Ventana
Cave, in southern Arizona on the Papago Indian Reservation, Haury (1950, cited in
S.Olsen 1985:81–82) reported dog remains, including one mummy of a small immature dog that was probably less than 1,000 years old and prepared by members of
the Hohokam culture. Other dog remains at the site were discovered in a layer that
radiocarbon dated to about 11,500 B.P. (ca. 9500 B.C.) (A-203) (Colton 1970:153),
though Stanley Olsen (1985:82) claimed that the age of the dogs is still unknown.

Though not quite on the scale of the Shang tombs, burials of dogs, some of
which were sacrificed, have been found in human graves at North American sites
dating as early as the Middle and Late Archaic periods. Included here are two well-
known sites, Eva in western Tennessee and Indian Knoll in western Kentucky. At
Eva the burials of 18 large dogs were discovered, four in flexed positions lying under
skulls of human burials. A total of 180 human burials were found at this Middle Archaic site, which dates to ca. 7200–5000 B.P. (ca. 5200–3000 B.C.) (Lewis and Lewis
1961). Similarly, at Indian Knoll, a Shell Mound Archaic site dating to about
5000–4000 B.P. (ca. 3000–2000 B.C.), 21 dog burials were excavated, in addition to
more than 1,000 human burials (Webb 1974). One question that has often been asked
at sites containing both human graves and combined dog-human interments is why
were some individuals buried with dogs while others were not? The answer is prob-

FIGURE 5.5   Mummies of two dogs from White Dog Cave, Arizona (from S. Olsen 1985:38).

ably related in part to the rank, status, clan membership, cause of death, age, and/or sex of the deceased (Strong 1985:37) and also to the possible spiritual role of the dog.

Another large Archaic cemetery, Port au Choix, is located along the west coast of Newfoundland's Great North Peninsula (see Figure 1.1). Here Tuck (1970) discovered nearly 100 human skeletons in 53 separate graves dating to the Maritime Archaic Tradition; the individuals laid to rest in these burials are referred to as the "Red Paint People" since red ocher pigment, similar to clay, accompanied many of them. Radiocarbon samples from the graves ranged in age between 2340 ± 110 B.C. at Locus II to 1280 ± 220 B.C. at Locus IV (about 4400–3500 B.P.). In Locus II one grave contained the skeletons of an adult man and woman lying on their sides facing each other, with the remains of an infant less than two years old held in the man's arms (Pferd 1987:51). Just above this deposit, Tuck found the skeletons of two large dogs, both placed on their sides with legs slightly bent in a flexed, or sleeping, position (Pferd 1987:52). One of the dogs presumably was killed by a blow to the left side of the head, as evidenced by a fractured skull, raising the possibility of a sacrificial act; the cause of death was not identified for the other dog. Pferd (1987:51) conjectured that the interment of these two dogs represented ceremonial offerings to accompany a family after death.

At around the same time as the Port au Choix cemetery (ca. 4000 B.P., 2000 B.C.), about 1,000 miles west in the northern part of the Finger Lakes area in New York, Laurentian Archaic Native Americans were also burying dogs with people (Ritchie 1945, 1980). One site in particular, Frontenac Island in Cayuga Lake, contained several fascinating finds. Excavating the site in 1939, 1940, and 1953, Ritchie (1945:7) unearthed 13 burials of what he believed to be two breeds of dogs: a smaller breed, perhaps the size of a terrier, consisting of 9 dogs; and a larger breed, resembling the size of a collie or shepherd, consisting of 3 dogs (the breed of the remaining dog, represented by an immature skeleton, could not be determined). According to Ritchie (1945:7), dog remains of the smaller breed had been carefully interred elsewhere in New York, including the Geneva and Oberlander sites, but only the Frontenac Island site had contained the remains of the larger breed.

Of the 13 dog burials discovered at the site, 6 were separate burials (4 small, 1 large, and 1 indeterminate), and the other 7 were found in human burials. In nearly every case, the dog skeleton lay curled up in a sleeping position. The remains of both breeds were placed in human graves: 5 small dogs associated with three extended and two flexed human skeletons and 2 large dogs associated with two extended human skeletons. In one feature six human burials were encountered with the remains of an immature dog. The dog was interred on a limestone slab, which was placed directly on top of the skeleton of an adult man. In all but 1 of the 7 dog-human burials at the Frontenac Island site, the dogs were interred with men and were usually accompanied by hunting and other equipment. Ritchie (1980:112) interpreted this pattern as recognition of invaluable services of the dog to the hunter. The other dog-human burial, which contained the remains of a puppy put directly on the neck of a flexed infant, also highlighted the importance of dogs in this Laurentian Archaic society. As Ritchie (1980:124) graphically described:

> This body [of the infant] had been buried in the probably still warm ashes of a hearth, an oyster-shell pendant lay on its chest, and a puppy of about the same size as the baby had been immolated and flexed directly upon it in intimate companionship.

This burial was not cremated, but cremation burials at Jamesport, Long Island, in New York contained mixed dog and human skeletal remains dating to the Orient phase of the Transitional Archaic period (ca. 3200 B.P., 1200 B.C.) (Ritchie 1959:56).

During the following Woodland period, mortuary ceremonialism of dogs among Native Americans reached its peak, based on archaeological evidence from a number of sites in the Northeast and elsewhere. Cantwell (1980) identified the occurrence of dog ceremonialism at several Middle Woodland sites in Illinois based on data from 30 dog burials at 14 sites: 27 dog burials at 13 Havana Tradition sites (ca. 2200–1600 B.P., 200 B.C.–A.D. 350), sometimes referred to as Illinois Hopewell, and

3 dog burials at an Allison Tradition site (ca. 2000–1600 B.P.). According to Cantwell (1980:480,490), a distinctive expression of the ritual relationship between dogs and people was seen in the following burial treatments: some dogs interred with elaborate grave goods, indicating considerable wealth (e.g., clay figurines, red ochre, copper bead, drilled bear-canine-tooth pendant, and various utilitarian tools); some in special tombs; some under house floors; and one rare secondary bundle burial, meaning that the dog remains had been previously buried, exhumed, and re-interred as a pile of disarticulated bones. Surprisingly, 27 of the 30 dog burials were found in living areas of the site apart from where people tended to be buried, and only one was placed in a human grave.

From the Frank Bay site in Ontario, dating to about 1000 B.P., Brizinski and Savage (1983) recovered the remains of 6 young dogs that they believed were ceremonially sacrificed, but presumably not eaten, and bundled for interment following a feast by the site's Algonquian inhabitants. In the 1978 excavation, all 6 dogs were found in a dismembered, unburnt condition. The presence of charred birch bark directly below 2 of the skeletons suggested that they were bundled in containers of this material. Red ochre accompanied 4 burials, and 1 contained a quartz crystal. The bundles were placed on top of a hearth that had been used to cook food as indicated by an abundance of charred bone refuse, possibly of beaver and muskrat. Radiocarbon samples from this refuse resulted in five dates that clustered around 1000 B.P. Evidence that the dogs were put to death is seen from cut marks on the bone, particularly on the cervical vertebrae or neck area. Also, cut marks were detected on a rib and some femura, or thigh bones of the hind leg; the cuts to the femura presumably were done to remove this portion of the legs from the hip sockets.

South of Frank Bay in the Great Lakes region of Michigan is another Woodland site that also contained a dog bundle burial, among other dog remains. The Juntunen site, located on Bois Blanc Island in the Straits of Mackinac, was excavated in 1960 by McPherron (1966), who recovered dog bones in all of the site's occupation phases, a period spanning roughly 1200–600 B.P. According to Prahl (1967:18), ceremonial use of the dog was represented by the inclusion of a dog's right and left legs, excluding the feet, in a "medicine bundle" associated with a human grave. Another unusual feature at the site consisted of a burial of a young dog associated with articulated skeletons (presumed burials) of a snowshoe hare and a bald eagle. In the Northeast archaeologists have also unearthed animal remains that were interred in prehistoric dog burials. For instance, at the Ridge Camp site on the Indian River in Milford, Connecticut, several dog burials were found. Interred together at the bottom of one refuse pit were the bodies of a human and a small dog, which was completely covered with fish scales of a large sturgeon (Rogers 1943:26–31). Also, at College Point in Queens, New York City, Lopez and Wisniewski (1958) reported a feature in which both a dog and a fisher, a small weasellike mammal, had been beheaded and buried. Kaeser (1970:30) believed that dog or other animal skeletons lacking heads (or tails) did not necessarily indicate ceremonial burial since butchering and skinning may have kept the head (and tail) attached to the skin as part of the pelt.

To the best of my knowledge, the largest number of dog skeletons (approximately 130) recovered from a Native American site comes from Weyanoke Old

Town, also called the Hatch site, in the tidewater region of Virginia (Blick, personal communication 1994). Although the site contains components dating back to at least the Early Archaic, all the dog burials are from the Late Woodland (Algonquian) village area of the site, dating to ca. A.D. 1400–1622 (about 550–330 B.P.). The dogs apparently were not eaten or skinned as the skeletal remains were usually found articulated, and none exhibited cut marks or other signs of butchery. Blick (1988) has written a preliminary report on osteometric analysis of 13 of the skeletal remains and has provided me with fascinating information, summarized below, on evidence of ceremonialism associated with some of the dog burials (personal communication 1994).

Most of the dogs were interred separately from human graves, but there were two cases of a male dog placed upside down on its back on top of a severed right human arm in two trash pit features. The necks of both dogs were contorted, and their paws were put (or had fallen) in such unusual positions to suggest that the dogs were originally buried with their feet in the air. Though the explanation is unclear, Blick speculated that the severed right arm represented the limbs of enemies, and the dogs were placed above them to keep the spirits of the owners at bay in the afterlife. In another feature, a large trash pit, were the remains of an elderly woman (about 60 years old) with a dog placed over her feet and covered with sherds from a broken pot. The dog was so tightly encircled in a flexed position that its snout was touching its pelvis, leading Blick to suspect that the dog may have been killed and put in the grave before the onset of *rigor mortis;* he also conceded the possibility that the dog died in its sleep in a tightly curled position. Situated slightly above this find were the remains of 5 immature dogs. Blick believed that the dogs were interred in this feature to accompany the spirit of the deceased woman into the afterlife.

During the Woodland period on Long Island and in the vicinity of New York City, dogs tended to be buried in domestic contexts near hearths and away from human graves, perhaps as symbolic watch dogs to protect the households (Strong 1985:36); a similar pattern was described by Cantwell (1980) for the Middle Woodland dog burials in Illinois. The number of dog interments associated with human burials increases for the Late Woodland period on Long Island and vicinity. This is especially true at the Archery Range site within Pelham Bay Park in the Bronx. Kaeser (1970) reported that this Late Woodland site contained the bones of at least 21 people, ranging in age from infancy to elderly, all of whom were interred as secondary bundle burials in an ossuary or mass grave. The remains of 3 dogs were also found associated with the feature; 2 were in bone bundles, and the third consisted of an articulated skeleton lying on its right side in a grave beneath the ossuary. Kaeser (1970:29) conjectured that the 2 bundle burials interred with human remains indicated that both dogs were probably valued by their masters, not only for hunting but also as camp guardians and companions. The third dog was apparently put to death by a blow to the skull as evidenced by bone fragments. Thus, Kaeser (1970:29) concluded that this dog was a sacrificial offering as part of a preliminary ceremonial burial preparatory to mass human interment.

Discoveries at three other Woodland sites on Long Island are also worthy of attention. One site near Port Washington excavated in 1900 by Harrington (1982) contained the remains of 14 dogs, 6 of which were placed in four separate human graves (three infants and an adult). One infant was interred with 3 dogs, whose bones were poorly preserved, and the other three human burials—two infants and an adult—each contained 1 dog. Harrington (1982, cited in Strong 1985:34) hypothesized three different methods of killing the latter 3 dogs: The dog in the adult burial was probably killed with a spear or arrow as a projectile point was lodged among its ribs; in light of the contorted position of the skeleton, the dog in one infant grave may have been buried alive and died while trying to dig its way out; and the dog in the other infant burial was possibly strangled as it showed no signs of violence. The second site is the Beach Haven site, located nearby. It was excavated in 1927 by Orchard (1977) and contained 2 dog burials, both placed in human graves. In 1 burial a small dog was interred near the bottom of a pit. About 30 cm above this deposit was a group of oyster shells set on edge about 13 cm apart in an oval pattern. About 60 cm above the shell oval the remains of an adult person were discovered buried in a flexed position and covered with apparent debris from a cooking hearth. The third site, located at Lake Montauk, was accidentally discovered by a construction crew in 1927 (Strong 1985:36). Latham conducted salvage work at the site and uncovered a wooden coffin containing an adult woman about 25 years old, a dog, and European trade goods, specifically, copper pots, glass beads, and pewter and clay smoking pipes, all dating to about 1670. As clearly indicated by this site, the Native American tradition of dog-human burial was still practiced on Long Island some 30 years after the establishment of European settlements there (Strong 1985:36).

Of all the identified dog burials in the coastal Northeast, many have been uncovered within and below prehistoric shell deposits. One of the earliest reports was made in 1895 by Calver (Finch 1909:70–71), who discovered intact skeletons of 3 dogs interred within thick shell features in the vicinity of 209th Street, near the Harlem River in north Manhattan. In light of the Lambert Farm dog burials, it is especially interesting that Calver found primarily oyster and clam shells surrounding and covering the skeletons and that many of the shells were unopened. Also, in 1907 Calver and Bolton (Bolton 1909:87–88) noted the bones of 3 puppies buried within both dense and shallow piles of shells along Seaman Avenue in Washington Heights (north Manhattan). Referring to these and other Native American sites discovered in Manhattan, Bolton as early as 1909 commented on the multifunctional purpose of prehistoric shell deposits:

> The use of shell pits partly for shells only, partly for the debris of feasts, partly for dog or fish burials and partly to cover human remains is a subject open to conjecture.

BOLTON 1909:93

On Grannis Island in New Haven, Connecticut, on the east shore of the Quinnipiac River, 5 or 6 dog interments were discovered in pits below prehistoric shell deposits (David Thompson, personal communication 1989). The dogs were buried in flexed positions lying on their sides. At least 1 was a juvenile. No radiocarbon dates exist from this site, which was excavated between 1940 and 1974 by the Greater New Haven Chapter of the Connecticut Archaeological Society. It is interesting to note that this site also contained disarticulated dog remains (Sargent 1952), which likely represent refuse from consumed meals. The assemblage is still being analyzed. At Squantum along Boston Harbor in eastern Massachusetts a complete skeleton of "an Eskimo dog" was found beneath a shell midden (Nelson 1989:29). A radiocarbon sample of the dog's ribs produced a corrected date of 1710 ± 70 B.P. (GX-13732).

At a site designated RI-972 on Potowomut Neck in Warwick, Rhode Island, about three miles southeast of Lambert Farm, I excavated a dog burial encountered within and beneath a thick shell feature also containing chipping debris and dense bone refuse (see Figure 1.2). A sample of quahog shells surrounding the articulated dog skeleton yielded an uncorrected radiocarbon date of 1180 ± 80 B.P. (Beta 10912) (Kerber, ed. 1984). The dog was interred in an extended position lying on its left side facing south. Only the dog's limbs and mandible were exposed and removed due to time and funding constraints. Until a radiocarbon sample of the dog's bones is dated, however, the association between the dog and the prehistoric shell deposit is uncertain.

The dog burial site that most resembles Lambert Farm is Sweet-Meadow Brook, also located in Warwick, just north of Apponaug Cove and only 1.2 miles northeast of Lambert Farm (see Figure 1.2). Sweet-Meadow Brook was excavated by Fowler (1956) in 1954 and 1955 with the Narragansett Archaeological Society (Morenon 1981). The site is multicomponent, spanning the Late Archaic and Woodland periods, based on recovered diagnostic artifacts. Like Lambert Farm, Sweet-Meadow Brook yielded abundant stone tools—including steatite platform smoking pipes— and numerous shell deposits of a variety of shellfish species. Seven thick shell features contained the skeletal remains of 8 people and 2 dogs. In one shell feature the bones of what Fowler (1956:5) called a "fairly large wolf-dog" were interred as a single grave. The remains of the other dog were encountered within a separate feature that also contained the skeletons of an adult man and woman and a four-year-old child. Associated with the remains of one person in the multiple burial feature was a steatite smoking pipe bowl fragment; two other platform pipes also were found at the site. The only uncorrected radiocarbon date for the site, 800 ± 80 B.P. (Lamont 270), came from a sample of oyster shells associated with one of the human burials and may be contemporaneous with the age of the 3 dog burials at Lambert Farm. Indeed, both sites may even have been settled by the same people, given their close proximity and striking similarities. The next section on ethnohistorical information on Native American dogs elucidates the various ways in which dogs were treated in life and death. The archaeological and ethnological material presented here provide clues to understanding why the Lambert Farm dogs were given such elaborate burials and how these prehistoric dogs could have been more than just pets to their Native American masters.

ETHNOHISTORICAL INFORMATION

Observations and descriptions recorded by European and American explorers, settlers, and travelers in the sixteenth through the eighteenth centuries provide a wealth of information on the many roles dogs played in Native American societies of the Northeast. Indeed, countless references to Native American dogs exist in the ethnohistorical records. While it is impossible to list all of them here, I will draw on a sample that represents several different ways that dogs served Native Americans in the region. Specifically, the data indicate these animals were treated as pets, hunting aides, religious sacrifices, emergency and ceremonial food supplies, spirit guardians, and afterlife companions.

Before discussing this topic, it is important to emphasize at the outset that the reporting of much historical information on Native Americans and their ways of life was affected by ethnocentric views of writers at the time. During the sixteenth through the eighteenth centuries, Native Americans and their cultures were commonly depicted as primitive, uncivilized, and savage, which made it difficult for Euro-American authors to provide objective accounts. In addition, early European explorers and settlers in the Northeast who recorded their interactions with Native Americans generally lacked an understanding of the different indigenous languages. Thus, even though considerable ethnohistorical evidence exists for various aspects of Native American culture in the region, one needs to be aware of its limitations. The mere fact that information is "in writing" does not necessarily mean it is unbiased.

Nevertheless, there is no doubt that Native Americans had dogs when the first Europeans arrived in northeastern North America in the sixteenth century. These animals were likely somewhat different in appearance from their prehistoric ancestors that were discussed in the previous section. Native American dogs across the continent had evolved into numerous varieties as a result of hundreds of years of interbreeding within their own species, with wolves, and probably with coyotes. Pferd (1987:9,10) claims that by the time Columbus landed in the Caribbean some 20 breeds of aboriginal dogs were widespread in the Americas, from Alaska in the far north to Tierra del Fuego at the tip of South America. Most of these breeds have disappeared. In North and Central America, for instance, the Mexican Chihuahua, Alaskan Malamute, and Eskimo dog are the only remaining native domesticated canines, though all three have undergone further changes due to modern dog breeders (Pferd 1987:9). In South America, Peru specifically, there are at least two breeds of native dogs. One is a hairless variety that, like the Chihuahua, was a food source. The other is a taller hunting-type dog (Quilter, personal communication 1995). Today, no breeds of Native American dogs still exist in the Northeast as they had interbred with European-introduced dogs over some 300 years. Before they vanished from the region, what were these historic Native American dogs like, and how were they treated by their masters? These and other related topics are addressed in the following pages.

One of the earliest written reports of Native American dogs was made on September 18, 1535, by the French explorer Cartier (1906:52), who saw three Huron men along the St. Lawrence River in Canada wearing capes and masks of "dogges skinnes white and blacke." Champlain, explorer of much of the northeastern coast, made the following observations in 1603, also among the Huron along the St. Lawrence River: They had many dogs for hunting; they slept next to their dogs; they danced "leaping about" with their dogs; and they rubbed their "greasy" hands on the hair of their dogs (1922:102,105). Sometime later, on another voyage between 1615 and 1618, Champlain (1929:129) mentioned that "dogs are in demand" at Native American banquets. Similarly, when the English explorer Hudson sailed up the Hudson River in 1610, he visited Mahicans, who killed a fat dog "at once," skinned it with shells "in great haste," and cooked and served it in his honor (de Laet 1909:49). Many other references to dogs as sacrifices and ceremonial food supplies exist in the records, as will be discussed shortly.

Another early report comes from the Pilgrims on November 15, 1620, when they were in what is now Provincetown on Cape Cod, prior to their famous landing in Plymouth. Captain Miles Standish noted seeing a dog with five or six Native Americans, who vanished into the woods and "whisled the Dogge after them" (Cheever 1848:32). Dutch explorers in 1625 observed that aboriginal dogs in southern New York were small. As indicated by van Wassenaer's (1909:80) somewhat biased passage, some Native Americans were "very much afraid" of a big Dutch dog that they encountered on a ship:

> . . . calling it, also, a sachem of dogs, as being one of the biggest. The dog, tied with a rope on board, was very ferocious against them, they being clad like beasts with skins, for he thought they were wild animals, but when they gave him some of their bread made of Indian corn, which grows there, he learned to distinguish them, that they were men.

Fridman (1989:65) claims that in early historical accounts indigenous dogs were rarely mentioned as being harnessed and used for sled traction in the Northeast. This is possibly because of their relatively small size. Elsewhere, however, larger dogs were harnessed and used for sled traction and for carrying packs. The latter is seen in Figure 5.3 among the Assiniboin from the northwestern Plains in the early twentieth century. One of the few North American archaeological sites that contains evidence of pack dogs is Keatley Creek, which is located in the Frasier River Valley of British Columbia and dates to between 2000 and 1000 B.P. (Hayden, personal communication 1995). At this site, Crellin (1994) observed deformities in the spines of two dogs, suggesting that both animals were exploited as beasts of burden.

Pring (1906:350), who explored the New England coast in 1603, observed that Native American dogs there had "sharpe and long noses." Based on his two voyages to New England in 1638–1639 and in 1663–1671, Josselyn (1988:67,133) noted that aboriginal dogs of the region were as common as in England, that they were "gallant" in hunting, and that Native Americans had obtained English dogs. According to Zeisberger (1910:31), by the late eighteenth century European dogs were "most commonly found among the Indians, especially the Delawares" of southern New York, New Jersey, eastern Pennsylvania, and northern Delaware. He added that in "former days" Native American dogs were more wolf-like, with ears that rose "rigidly from the head" (Zeisberger 1910:31). Farther north, the Micmac dogs of Nova Scotia, New Brunswick, and eastern Quebec, as described by Lescarbot (1914, vol. 3:221) in the early seventeenth century, were similar to "foxes in form and size, and with hair of all colours." Denys (1908:430) also stated that for these people during the seventeenth century "their wealth was in proportion to their dogs."

An especially rich source of early historical information on Native Americans is the *Jesuit Relations* (Thwaites 1896–1901), annual reports written from 1610 until 1791 by French Jesuit missionaries in New France (including present-day southeastern Canada and the Great Lakes region). Some of the major tribal groups that occupied this geographic area and that are discussed in the reports include Algonquian speakers (e.g., Montagnais, Micmacs, Abenakis, and Ottawas) and Iroquoian speakers (e.g., Hurons and the Five Nation Iroquois Confederacy) (Thwaites 1896:10–11).

It appears that there was no shortage of dogs among these Native Americans as reported by the Jesuits, including Father le Jeune (1634a, in Thwaites vol. 7:43) who described dogs as "large and numerous." On cold winter nights dogs probably were welcomed as sleeping companions, providing warmth from their body heat. Indeed, le Jeune (1634a, in Thwaites vol. 7:43,45) gave the following graphic description of the close living quarters in one house in which he had slept among the Montagnais of the upper St. Lawrence River:

> As to the dogs, which I have mentioned as one of the discomforts of the Savages' houses, I do not know that I ought to blame them, for they have sometimes rendered me good service. . . . These poor beasts, not being able to live outdoors, came and lay down upon my shoulders, sometimes upon my feet, and as I only had one blanket to serve both as covering and mattress, I was not sorry for this protection, willingly restoring to them a part of the heat I drew from them. . . . These animals, being famished, as they have nothing to eat any more than we do, do nothing but run to and fro gnawing at everything in the cabin. . . . They have often upset for me my bark dish, and all it contained, in my gown. . . . There was not one of us who did not hold his plate down with both hands on the ground, which serves as table, seat, and bed to both men and dogs.

Father de Crépieul (1697, in Thwaites vol. 65:45) wrote that on his overnight visits to Montagnais villages he usually awoke surrounded by dogs, sometimes as many as 10.

Many of the Jesuit accounts mentioned that dogs were commonly used in hunting and tracking various animals, including beavers and bears (le Jeune 1634b, in Thwaites vol. 6:299; le Mercier 1637a, in Thwaites vol. 14:33). Also, Father Lalemant (1647, in Thwaites vol. 32:27) observed that Algonquians near Montreal regularly brought along a female dog on scouting patrols to pick up the scent of their Iroquois enemies. During the seventeenth century, according to Denys (1908:429), every Micmac hunter had 7 or 8 dogs. In several instances among Native Americans in New France, taboos were described against allowing dogs to eat certain animals in order to ensure successful hunting. The most frequently cited creature on this list was beaver, but fish, deer, moose, birds, and porcupines also were mentioned among the animal bones that were not thrown to dogs (de Brébeuf 1636, in Thwaites vol. 10:167; le Jeune 1634b, in Thwaites vol. 6:211). These bones were thrown instead into a fire or a river or even buried so the dogs could not find them (Anonymous 1658, in Thwaites vol. 44:303). Since other animals were considered "devoid of intelligence," their bones were "held in contempt" and thus thrown to the dogs (Anonymous 1658, in Thwaites vol. 44:303). Speck (1925:58–59) reported that a "wolf-dog" was still used in hunting as recently as 1925 among the Montagnais and Naskapi of the Gulf of St. Lawrence region. It is especially noteworthy that these

Native Americans did not give caribou bones to their dogs for fear of bad luck in subsequent hunts. As Speck (1925:64) argued:

> It is their belief that the game animals are sensitive to ill-treatment of the parts left over after the flesh had been eaten. The spirits of the animals resent in particular the ignominy of seeing their bones fought over, crunched, and devoured by dogs, because the dog, an animal like themselves, has turned traitor to his kind, and living with man, aids him in following their traces and bringing them down.

It is also conceivable that dogs were not fed certain animal meat for fear that they might choke on the bones. Indeed, Spiess and Lewis (1995:349) believed such was the case approximately 4400 B.P. at Turner Farm, an enormous shell midden located on North Haven Island in Penobscot Bay in Maine. Containing what is probably the longest and most complex sequence on the Gulf of Maine Coast, this site spans nearly five millennia from about 5000 B.P. to the early historic period (Bourque 1995:13,19). Dogs were present at Turner Farm at least during the Late Archaic period, specifically, both the Moorehead phase (Occupation 2 at the site) and the Susquehanna Tradition (Occupation 3 at the site), based on the recovery of several dog burials and disarticulated dog remains. A charcoal sample from only one dog burial was radiocarbon dated to 4390 ± 55 B.P. (SI 1921) (Bourque 1995:42–43); this was one of six dog burials discovered in Occupation 2. Worthy of emphasis is the identification of an area, so-called Area 2 (associated with Occupation 2), in which dogs were presumably fed by prehistoric Native Americans at Turner Farm. Spiess and Lewis (1995:349) made this interpretation based on the low proportion of fish bone and bird bone and the high proportion of seal bone in Area 2. In other parts of the site, where dogs supposedly were given few or no food scraps, fish and bird remains were much more abundant, and seal bone was scarce and less clustered than in Area 2. The authors reasoned that since bones of fish and birds are notorious for choking dogs, people probably avoided feeding dogs carcasses of these animals. Instead, it is likely that seal meat was the choice dog food at Turner Farm because people favored it less than other meat, as indicated by ethnographic observations (Spiess and Lewis 1995:349). That seal meat was fed to the dogs is further supported by the ragged ends exhibited on many of the seal bones in Area 2, apparently due to dog chewing.

Returning to the Jesuit accounts, the vast majority of references to Native American dogs pertained to the interrelated role of religious sacrifice, afterlife companion, and ceremonial food supply. Indeed, one of the first references was made in 1612 by Father Biard, who observed among the Micmacs a *tabagie,* or solemn banquet to honor a dying man's last farewell. As described by Biard (1612, in Thwaites vol. 2:17):

> The farewell and the mourning are finished by the slaughter of dogs, that the dying man may have forerunners in the other world. This slaughter is accompanied by the *tabagie* and what follows—namely, the singing and dancing.

Biard (1616, in Thwaites vol. 3:127) added that the sacrificed dogs were often cooked and eaten at the *tabagie,* which also had come to be called a dog feast. If the dogs were not eaten, they were buried with the dead man and all that he owned (Biard 1616, in Thwaites vol. 3:131). The consumption of dog meat by Native Americans outside of ritual occasions was rarely noted by the Jesuits and other authors. One example is the report by Mary Rowlandson, who was captured by Wampanoags of southeastern Massachusetts during King Philip's War in 1675–1676 and observed these people eating dogs to stay alive (Drake 1884:54, cited in Butler and Hadlock 1949:21).

Dog feasts, as reported by the Jesuits, were held for reasons other than a *tabagie*. Butler and Hadlock (1949:22) maintained that eating dog flesh was an important part of ceremonies intended to avert sickness or other misfortune and in preparation for war, as well as death. For instance, Father le Mercier (1637b, in Thwaites vol. 13:31,33), among several other Jesuits, made reference to a Huron shaman or medicine man who prescribed a dog feast to cure sick individuals, both young and old. Le Mercier (1637b, in Thwaites vol. 13:43,45) also wrote that a dog feast was held in a Huron village for an Iroquois captive, who received a large portion of the cooked dog. Father Lalemant told of a Huron man who dreamt that the Iroquois had burned him in captivity. In order to prevent this from actually occurring, the man participated in a ceremony that concluded by killing a dog, which was then "singed and roasted in the flames, and . . . eaten at a public feast, in the same manner as they usually eat their Captives" (Lalemant 1642, in Thwaites vol. 23:173). According to Fenton (1953:106–7), Huron, Mohawk, and Oneida during the seventeenth century held war feasts prior to engaging in a battle. As part of the ceremony, the head of an animal, often a dog, was cooked in soup and presented to the leader and the most distinguished warriors. The dog provided much ritualistic meaning in the ceremony, as interpreted by Fenton (1978:316):

> War feasts were far from acts of piety. Seeing the kettle and the steaming platters of dog meat, which symbolized the broth and flesh of captives that they would later drink and eat, transported the beholders into fits of rage and fury as they mentioned their enemies in songs and compared them to dogs.

Sacrificed dogs, however, frequently were not consumed, particularly when attempts were made to ward off disease, which was increasingly reported by the Jesuits after 1666. In one such situation Father Marest (1712, in Thwaites vol. 66:241) described the sacrifice of 40 dogs by shamans to halt a fatal illness that had decimated a Mascouten village near Lake Michigan. Other dog sacrifices were performed to appease lightning storms (Gravier 1694, in Thwaites vol. 64:187). Often the sacrificed dogs that were not eaten were suspended from the tops of long poles placed in Native American villages (Dablon 1677, in Thwaites vol. 60:227). Putting the bodies of sacrificed dogs on poles also was practiced by the Koryak along the Russian Pacific Coast, as well as by some Native American groups in the Northwest Coast region of the United States and southern Canada (Hayden 1995:84). Indeed, Hayden (1995:87, personal communication 1995) suggested that the practice of displaying sacrificed dogs on poles occurred between 2,000 and 1,000 years ago at Keatley Creek in British Columbia, though he admitted the lack of definite proof. The basis of his interpretation was twofold: At least one dog skull showed evidence of a killing blow to the head; and one or two dog skulls were weathered, indicating exposure over some time outside (Hayden 1995:86–87, personal communication 1995). Hayden went further to argue that the raising of dogs by complex prehistoric hunters and gatherers of the Northwest Coast was part of status competition. As he explained, dogs were kept, bred, and sacrificed as a form of prestige display at dog feasts to symbolize the amount of control the host, often a chief, had over labor and to enhance greatly the host's status (Hayden 1990:41-2, 1995:87).

Despite the consumption and sacrifice of dogs in the Northeast, these animals were still treated affectionately by Native Americans. Lalemant (1639, in Thwaites vol. 17:13,15) wrote that Huron dogs were "held as dear as the children of the house, and share the beds, plates, and food of their masters." In addition, le Mercier offered this poignant description of how deeply a Huron mourned his dog after it was killed pursuing a bear. In the owner's translated words:

> Ah! it is true . . . that I dearly loved Ouatit [name of dog]; I had resolved to keep him with me all his life; there was no dream that could have influenced me to make a feast of him,—I would not have given him for anything in the world.

LE MERCIER 1637A, IN THWAITES VOL. 14:35

In 1623 or 1624 Sagard (1939:128) observed Huron women feeding puppies, too young to take solid foods, in the same manner that the men fed their infants whose mothers had died—by filling one's mouth with water in which corn had boiled and putting the puppy's or baby's mouth against one's own to make it swallow the liquid. Similarly, among the Micmac during the seventeenth century, dogs were also so highly cherished that "if they have little ones which the mother cannot nourish, the women suckle them; when they are large they are given soup" (Denys 1908:430).

Perhaps the best known historic case of dog sacrifice in the Northeast is the ritual burning of a white dog by the Iroquois in New York during the seven-day religious celebration called the Midwinter Festival. Morgan (1851) observed this annual ceremony in about 1846 among the Seneca in western New York, probably at the Sand Hill Longhouse on the Tonawanda Reservation (Tooker 1970:106,135). The Midwinter Festival traditionally ushered in the new year and usually began about the first of February. On the first day of the celebration, a white dog was strangled, being "careful neither to shed his blood, nor break his bones" (Morgan 1851:210). A white dog was selected because "white was the Iroquois emblem of purity and of faith" (Morgan 1851:210). After it was killed, the dog was spotted with red paint, ornamented with feathers, and around its neck was hung a string of white wampum (cut shell beads strung on a dozen or more 3-foot-long strands). Once decorated, the dead animal was suspended about 8 feet above the ground on a pole and left there until the fifth day. The most prominent act of the celebration was the burning of the dog, which occurred on the fifth day and was accompanied by many ceremonies followed by a feast. Morgan (1851:216–17) described in detail what he believed was the religious significance of the dog cremation:

> . . . the simple idea of the sacrifice was, to send up the spirit of the dog as a messenger to the Great Spirit, to announce their (Iroquois) continued fidelity to his service, and, also, to convey to him their united thanks for the blessings of the year. The fidelity of

the dog, the companion of the Indian, as a hunter, was emblematical of their fidelity. No messenger so trusty could be found to bear their petitions to the Master of life. . . . This sacrifice was the most solemn and impressive manner of drawing near to the Great Spirit known to the Iroquois. They used the spirit of the dog in precisely the same manner that they did the incense of tobacco, as an instrumentality through which to commune with their Maker. This sacrifice was their highest act of piety.

Morgan (1851) further argued that the Midwinter Festival involving the dog-burning ritual was an Iroquois tradition that went back many generations among the Seneca, Mohawk, Oneida, Onondaga, and Cayuga. It is especially interesting to note a reference in the *Jesuit Relations* from 1636 of "a white dog, to make a feast with it and to seek information by it" (le Jeune 1636, in Thwaites vol. 8:125); the Native American group was not specified for this reference. Today the burning of a white dog as part of the Midwinter Festival is no longer practiced by the Five Nation Iroquois Confederacy. Its last occurrence was reported toward the end of the nineteenth century among the Seneca (Tooker 1970:46).

Farther south, Tantaquidgeon (1942) recorded the traditional folk medicine of the Delaware. Instead of sacrificing their dogs, these Native Americans attempted to prolong the lives of dogs and people by using dogs as guardians of health. As dictated in 1930 by a Delaware, called Wi-tapanóxwe ("Walks with Daylight"), to Tantaquidgeon (1942:36):

Upon the birth of a Delaware child, it was given a pet to serve as the guardian of its health. If there was sickness about, the Delaware believed that it would be visited upon the dog instead of its little master. The animal was thought to say, 'I am only a dog, the child is more precious.' A small bag containing charcoal was tied around the pet animal's neck by the child's parents. Frequently they would talk to the dog. If the animal died, it was buried and the child given another pet. However, if the child fell sick and died, a release ceremony was performed by placing a string of wampum about its neck, thus freeing the animal.

Lastly, among the Narragansett in Rhode Island, there is little mention of dogs in the early ethnohistorical records. Williams (1973), who recorded in 1643 a considerable amount of information on his interactions with the Narragansett, referred to dogs only a few times: in his chapter on hunting (1973:224) and in noting four variations of the word for dog, which in the Cowweset dialect was "Anùm" (1973:174). This word may have been spoken by the prehistoric residents of Lambert Farm. Chapin (1920:5) pointed out that in 1644 and 1660 some Narragansetts used rough drawings of dogs as personal signature marks on English legal documents. This may have implied an element of guardianship, as interpreted by Fridman (1989:183), if the mark of the dog was intended to protect its owner against the non–Native Americans with whom an agreement was supposedly reached.

These are just some of the many ethnohistorical and archaeological references to dogs in the Northeast and elsewhere. Far from exhaustive, this list still encompasses the various ways in which dogs were treated in historic and prehistoric Native American societies. We return to Lambert Farm in the next chapter, the conclusion of the book.

CHAPTER 6

Conclusion

The previous review of ethnohistorical material on Native American dogs in the Northeast indicates that these domesticated animals embodied a duality. In Cantwell's (1980:491) words:

> . . . dogs are interstitial, that is intermediate between the forest, the world of animals, and the camp, the world of men. Like men they travel between the two worlds, but the dogs belong to neither and are, in that sense, liminal to both. Small wonder then that dogs appear in ritual contexts, as parts of ritual meals, as sacrifices, as totems, as mediators with the spirit world, as grave goods with humans, or . . . buried as humans are where humans live.

This heightened symbolic, ritualistic, and ceremonial usage of dogs, according to Strong (1985:32–33), undoubtedly was influenced by the practical role these creatures played in everyday village life. They provided protection, companionship, hunting assistance, an emergency supply of meat, and even clothing to many historic Native American groups. At the same time the data suggest that dogs also functioned as intermediaries, messengers, and guides between this world and the spirit world (Strong 1985:33).

As an aside, it is interesting to compare briefly the role of dogs in historic and prehistoric Native American societies with that of American society today. In the United States dogs are primarily kept as pets and, as such, tend to be cherished by their owners. However, we do not think of dogs as sacred creatures that fulfill symbolic or ceremonial roles. And we certainly do not consider dogs edible. Indeed, the mere thought would disgust most Americans. But according to Leach (1964), it is precisely because of this view that dogs are regarded as sacred in contemporary English (and presumably American) society. As Leach (1964:33) explained, the sacredness of dogs is manifested, in part, by the cultural rule, or taboo, that forbids consuming dog meat. Because of this taboo, dogs possess ritual value, in Leach's (1964:30) words. That is to say they have a special power. Why do we refuse to eat dogs and, in fact, find the idea repulsive? Leach (1964:32) claimed that this disgust is largely a matter of verbal categories. In colloquial English there are contexts in which dogs and people are equated. They are "companions" of one another; the dog is "man's best friend." But since people and food are antithetical categories, and people and dogs are equated, it follows that dogs cannot be food in our society (Leach 1964:32). Put another way, by refusing to eat dog meat, we enforce the rule that forbids cannibalism.

Concerning the rich body of historical information that was discussed in the preceding chapter, how can we use this material to interpret dog remains from archaeological sites in the Northeast and Lambert Farm, in particular? The answer to this question is mixed. While ethnohistorical data on Native American dogs provide considerable insight into the role of these animals, and it is tempting to apply the information to archaeological cases in reaching definitive conclusions, the material should only be used as a basis for speculation. Speculation may be presented explicitly as such, or it may take the form of hypotheses that would then need to be tested against specific archaeological data. Interestingly, this precise issue was raised some 100 years ago when Calver (Bolton 1909:87; Finch 1909:71) reasoned in 1895 that prehistoric dog burials he observed in Manhattan were evidence of ceremonial sacrifices in connection with the Iroquoian "White Dog Feast." On the other hand, Skinner (1909:233), noting both the noncremated condition and the Algonquian affiliation of these burials, argued that "it seems more probable that such burials are simply those of pet animals, interred as we to-day honor a faithful dog."

Returning to Lambert Farm, it is likely that the dogs at this site functioned in many of the ways summarized in the previous chapter. But at this time we can only speculate as to the exact nature of these roles. My "best guess" is presented here, though this conjecture admittedly may not be subject to the scientific rigors of hypothesis testing. I believe that the Lambert Farm dogs played a utilitarian role in life and a ritualistic one in death. At present, there is no reason to refute the possibility that all three dogs were pets. It is likely that the adult dog, because of its advanced age, provided companionship to one or several people and assisted members of the settlement in tracking game, especially deer. The puppies would have been too young for both of these practical roles. Whether the three dogs were well cared for and regularly fed by the people of Lambert Farm is unknown. Even though the adult dog lived for some five or six years, once weened it could have survived by scavenging refuse from human meals, as opposed to having been fed. The same is true for both puppies.

The ritualistic role of the three dogs is suggested by their interment in the two large, buried shell mounds among food remains and cultural debris. The considerable effort expended in producing these conspicuous features indicates the importance of these three dogs within mortuary contexts, which may reflect whatever importance the dogs had in life. We will never know precisely why the dogs were interred in this manner, but it is easy to surmise that their burials were associated with ceremonial activities, including feasting, smoking, and dancing, in similar ways to those described previously in ethnohistorical records. Although there is no direct evidence that the dogs were sacrificed, the age of the puppies raises suspicion of such an occurrence, which would be consistent with their unusual burial treatment and the inferred ritual surrounding their interment.

Two additional points should be discussed here. First, several disarticulated dog remains at Lambert Farm were recovered from shell features, along with other food remains. As mentioned earlier, some of these bones could have been displaced from dog burials due to plowing and other disturbances. On the other hand, I believe many, if not all, of these disarticulated skeletal remains represent consumed meals of dogs. If so, why were these dogs eaten and not buried, while at least three other dogs were buried but not eaten? I think the answer is related to the ritualistic role of Native American dogs at Lambert Farm. Eating dogs could be seen in purely economic terms as an emergency supply of meat, which is ethnohistorically supported elsewhere. But at Lambert Farm food apparently was plentiful and regularly available without the addition of dog meat to the diet. Thus, it is conceivable that the consumption of dogs at the site was done in a ceremonial context, as we have seen in the previous ethnohistorical accounts of other Native American groups. Unfortunately, what is much more difficult to surmise concerns the specific ritual(s) at which dogs were eaten and why dogs were on the menu.

The second point is that the three dog burials were not associated with human skeletal remains, unlike many other prehistoric Native American burials in the region, nor were any human burials discovered at Lambert Farm. It is possible, though unlikely, that human burials existed within the area of the site that we investigated, specifically, between our test units and thus were not discovered. Similarly, most of the dead could have been buried away from the site area that we excavated. Wherever these burials are located, it is plausible that some also contain the articulated remains of dogs. Even without any evidence that Lambert Farm dogs and people were interred together and that the three buried dogs were sacrificed, we can still speculate that the deaths and burials of the three dogs marked the demise or illness of one or more of the site's residents in ways reported by ethnohistorical observations.

While dogs played important roles in numerous Native American societies, clearly, life did not revolve around canines. This is as true at Lambert Farm as it is at any archaeological site. The picture of Native American life at Lambert Farm that emerges from the excavation and from some "educated guesses" is similar to what occurred at many other prehistoric sites in southern New England. We know that various people inhabited Lambert Farm during the past 5,000 years or so of prehistory. The most intense settlement occurred during the Late Woodland period, between about 1000 and 450 B.P. People camped at the site during all times of the year, possibly in groups ranging between a few and more than 50 individuals. Some groups may have stayed for only a few days, others for a few seasons or even a few years. Some groups probably returned to Lambert Farm year after year, but all eventually moved elsewhere in their regular pursuit of food. They survived by hunting animals, fishing, and gathering wild plants and shellfish. All of these resources could have been obtained within a 30-minute walk from the site during particular seasons. The various residents of Lambert Farm did not grow domesticated crops, such as corn, beans, and squash, nor did they establish long-term permanent villages at the site. While these people, at least during the Late Woodland period, are the ancestors of the Narragansett Indians who live in Rhode Island today, we do not know exactly what they were like. However, a description of the Narragansetts made by Verrazzano during his exploration of Narragansett Bay in the spring of 1524 provides a vivid image:

> These people are the most beautiful and have the most civil customs that we have found on this voyage. They are taller than we are . . . the face is clear-cut . . . the eyes are black and alert, and their manner is sweet and gentle, very like the manner of the ancients.
>
> WROTH 1970:138

If we select a specific settlement at Lambert Farm, one that occurred on a "typical" summer day during the Late Woodland period (as much evidence exists from this time at the site), we can imagine the following, based partly on ethnohistorical information on Narragansett life during the seventeenth century (Simmons 1978; Williams 1973).

Some 30 men, women, and children lived at the site. Except the young children, all wore loinclothes made of animal skins. Each family slept in one of six closely spaced conical wigwams, which measured 6 meters in diameter and were built of poles placed in the ground. The bent poles were laced inwardly and were covered with overlapping sheets of bark or mats made of grass. At the apex of the wigwam, directly above a fire set in a circular, stone-lined hearth, was an opening to vent the smoke. Around the periphery of the structure were sleeping platforms. In one wigwam sat a shaman, as he attempted to heal an infirm old man. Outside, smoke from many hearths filled the air, though not all hearths had active fires. Clams were steaming at some hearths, while deer meat was cooking at others. At a large hearth covered by wooden scaffolds, two women were preserving meat by smoking and drying. Several mounds and pits containing rotting food refuse were scattered across the site. In one pit preserved food was being stored for the lean winter months ahead. Close by, a man was butchering a deer carcass, as another was making and resharpening stone tools. Hundreds of quartz flakes littered this spot and many others. A woman was using a pot to draw water from the spring at the eastern edge of the camp. Earlier that day she and her two teenage daughters had travelled a considerable distance to obtain clay for pottery and grass for mats and baskets that they were making.

Sounds of babies crying, children laughing, and adults talking were heard throughout the site. Seven dogs could be seen in the camp, including three puppies playing with children. Not everyone was at the camp today. A few men and a dog had left yesterday to hunt deer some 5 kilometers away and were expected tomorrow. Also, several women and a few older children were nearby gathering berries and other wild plants. Later, they will walk down the path to Apponaug Cove to collect shellfish; they will be joined there by a few men working on a dugout canoe along the beach. All would be returning by late afternoon, most likely with a few baskets of clams. Much of the land surrounding the camp, including the area between the camp and the coast, was previously cleared of trees so that firewood could be collected and the new growth could attract game, especially deer. One could see the shore, more than a kilometer away, and smoke from several campfires at farther distances.

This is just one of the many plausible scenarios for what Native American daily life was like at Lambert Farm and for what the site looked like during one of its occupations. Obviously, this is a limited sketch that cannot possibly depict the complexity and full range of behavior, much of which also occurred at other archaeological sites. Nevertheless, it can still be concluded from several perspectives that Lambert Farm is an extraordinary cultural resource. Although the site has now been destroyed by residential development, the intensive research conducted prior to construction succeeded in recovering an enormous quantity of archaeological materials, including the numerous tools, well-preserved food remains, and other diverse objects. The site also contained rare discoveries, especially the dog burials, and the only radiocarbon-dated skeletal remains of domesticated dog in Rhode Island.

Not only is Lambert Farm extraordinary, but so is the realization that none of the site's 56,838 cultural remains would have been recovered, cleaned, catalogued, analyzed, interpreted, reported on, and preserved without the voluntary cooperation, concerted effort, and generous support provided by hundreds of individuals, including state and city officials, developers, archaeologists, granting agencies, and, most important, the general public. Yet despite the wealth of information collected from this prolific archaeological site, we are left with many more questions than answers. It may be trite to mention, but it truly seems to have been the case, despite (or perhaps, ironically, due to) the large-scale testing performed at Lambert Farm—the more we uncovered, the more we realized how little we knew about the site and its Native American inhabitants. Lambert Farm's vast assemblage of cultural remains has just begun to be studied. With the completion of further analyses of the collection, especially the dog burials and their associated shell features, and additional research at nearby sites, we hope to learn even more about Lambert Farm and how it fits into the larger picture of prehistoric human life in the region.

REFERENCES

Allen, G. M. 1920. Dogs of the American Aborigines. *Bulletin of the Museum of Comparative Zoology at Harvard College* 63(9):431–517.

Anonymous. 1658. Relation of What Occurred Most Remarkable in the Missions of the Fathers of the Society of Jesus in New France in the Years 1657 and 1658. In Thwaites, ed. 1899, 44:133–317.

Anyang Archaeological Team (Institute of Archaeology, Chinese Academy of Social Sciences). 1979. 1969–1977 Nian Yinxu Xiqu Muzang Fajue Baogao. *Kaogu Xuebao*, No. 1:27–146. Beijing.

Barber, R. J. 1983. Diversity in Shell Middens: The View from Morrill Point. *Man in the Northeast* 25:109–25.

Barton, B. S. 1803. On Indian Dogs. *The Philosophical Magazine* 15(57):1–9, 136–43.

Bernabo, J. C. 1977. *Sensing Climatically and Culturally Induced Environmental Change Using Palynological Data.* Ph.D. Dissertation, Geological Sciences, Brown University, Providence.

Bernstein, D. J. 1987. *Prehistoric Subsistence at Greenwich Cove, Rhode Island.* Ph.D. Dissertation, Anthropology, State University of New York, Binghamton. Ann Arbor, University Microfilms.

Bernstein, D. J. 1993. *Prehistoric Subsistence on the Southern New England Coast: The Record from Narragansett Bay.* San Diego: Academic Press.

Biard, P. 1612. Lettre au R.P. Provincial, à Paris. In Thwaites, ed. 1896, 2:4–55.

Biard, P. 1616. Relation of New France, of Its Lands, Nature of the Country, and of Its Inhabitants. In Thwaites, ed. 1897, 3:21–283.

Blick, J. P. 1988. A Preliminary Report on the Osteometric Analysis of Some Aboriginal Dogs *(Canis familiaris)* from Weyanoke Old Town, 44 PG 51, Prince George County, Virginia. *Quarterly Bulletin of the Archeological Society of Virginia* 43(1):1–13.

Blukis Onat, A. R. 1985. The Multifunctional Use of Shellfish Remains: From Garbage to Community Engineering. *Northwest Anthropological Research Notes* 19(1):201–7.

Bolton, R. P. 1909. The Indians of Washington Heights. In *The Indians of Greater New York and the Lower Hudson*, ed. C. Wissler, pp. 74–109. *Anthropological Papers of the American Museum of Natural History*, Vol. III. New York: Hudson-Fulton.

Bourque, B. J. 1995. *Diversity and Complexity in Prehistoric Maritime Societies: A Gulf of Maine Perspective.* New York: Plenum Press.

Braun, D. P. 1974. Explanatory Models for the Evolution of Coastal Adaptation in Prehistoric New England. *American Antiquity* 39:582–96.

Brébeuf, J. de. 1636. Relation of What Occurred in the Country of the Hurons in the Year 1636. In Thwaites, ed. 1897, 10:5–317.

Brizinski, M., and H. Savage. 1983. Dog Sacrifices among the Algonkian Indians: An Example from the Frank Bay Site. *Ontario Archaeology* 39:33–40.

Butler, E., and W. S. Hadlock. 1949. Dogs of the Northeastern Woodland Indians. *Bulletin of the Massachusetts Archaeological Society* 10(2):17–35.

Cantwell, A. M. 1980. Middle Woodland Dog Ceremonialism in Illinois. *The Wisconsin Archeologist* 61(4):480–96.

Cardozo, C. (ed.). 1993. *Native Nations: First Americans as Seen by Edward S. Curtis.* Boston: Little, Brown and Co.

Cartier, J. 1906. A Shorte and Briefe Narration 1535–1536. In *Early English and French Voyages, 1534–1608,* ed. H.S. Burrage, pp. 37–88. New York: Charles Scribner's Sons.

Ceci, L. 1979. Maize and Cultivation in Coastal New York: The Archaeological, Agronomical, and Documentary Evidence. *North American Archaeologist* 1:45–74.

Ceci, L. 1990. Radiocarbon Dating 'Village Sites' in Coastal New York: Settlement Pattern Change in the Middle to Late Woodland. *Man in the Northeast* 39:1–28.

Champlain, S. de. 1922. *The Works of Samuel de Champlain, Vol. I: 1599–1607.* Tran. and ed. by H. H. Langton and W. F. Ganong. Toronto: The Champlain Society.

Champlain, S. de. 1929. *The Works of Samuel de Champlain, Vol. III: 1615–1618.* Tran. and ed. by H. H. Langton and W. F. Ganong. Toronto: The Champlain Society.

Chapin, H. M. 1920. *Dogs in Early New England.* Providence: E.A. Johnson & Co.

Cheever, G. B. 1848 [1622]. *The Journal of the Pilgrims at Plymouth in New England, in 1620.* New York: John Wiley.

Claassen, C. 1991. Gender, Shellfishing, and the Shell Mound Archaic. In Gero and Conkey, eds. 1991:276–300.

Clutton-Brock, J. 1987. *A Natural History of Domesticated Mammals.* Austin: University of Texas Press.

Clutton-Brock, J., and N. Noe-Nygaard. 1990. New Osteological and C-Isotope Evidence on Mesolithic Dogs: Companions to Hunters and Fishers at Star Carr, Seamer Carr, and Kongemose. *Journal of Archaeological Science* 17:643–53.

Colton, H. S. 1970. The Aboriginal Southwestern Indian Dog. *American Antiquity* 35(2):153–59.

Crellin, D. F. 1994. *Is There a Dog in the House: The Cultural Significance of Prehistoric Domesticated Dogs in the Mid Fraser River Region of British Columbia.* M.A. Thesis, Archaeology, Simon Fraser University.

Crépieul, F. de. 1697. The Life of a Montagnaix Missionary, Presented to His Successors in the Montagnaix Mission for Their Instruction and Greater Consolation. In Thwaites, ed. 1900, 65:43–49.

Cronan, J. M. 1968. *The Mammals of Rhode Island.* Wildlife Pamphlet No. 6. Providence: Rhode Island Department of Natural Resources.

Dablon, C. 1677. Relation of What Occurred Most Remarkable in the Missions of the Fathers of the Society of Jesus in New France in the Years 1676 and 1677. In Thwaites, ed. 1900, 60:169–309.

Darwin, C. 1868. *The Variation of Animals and Plants under Domestication.* New York: Appleton.

Davis, S. J. M. 1987. *The Archaeology of Animals.* London: B. T. Batsford Ltd.

Davis, S. J. M., and F. R. Valla. 1978. Evidence for Domestication of the Dog 12,000 Years Ago in the Natufian of Israel. *Nature* 276(5688):608–10.

DeForest, J. W. 1852. *History of the Indians of Connecticut from the Earliest Known Period to 1850.* Hartford: Hamersley.

Degerbøl, M. 1961. On a Find of a Preboreal Domestic Dog *(Canis familiaris)* from Star Carr, Yorkshire, with Remarks on Other Mesolithic Dogs. *Proceedings of the Prehistoric Society* 27(3):35–55.

Densmore, F. 1928. *Uses of Plants by the Chippewa Indians.* Forty-fourth Annual Report of the Bureau of American Ethnology. Washington, D.C.: Smithsonian Institution.

Densmore, F. 1929. *Chippewa Customs.* Bureau of American Ethnology, Bulletin 86. Washington, D.C.: Smithsonian Institution.

Denys, N. 1908 [1672]. *The Description and Natural History of the Coasts of North America* (Acadia), tran. and ed. by W. F. Ganong. Toronto: The Champlain Society.

Donahue, D. J. 1994. Facsimile transmission to Jordan Kerber, Department of Sociology and Anthropology, Colgate University, Hamilton, New York. January 25.

Drake, S. G. 1884. *Tragedies of the Wilderness*. Boston: Antiquarian Bookstore and Institute.

Eaton, G. F. 1898. The Prehistoric Fauna of Block Island (R.I.) as Indicated by Its Ancient Shell-Heaps. *American Journal of Science*, Fourth Series, 6:137–59.

Elias, T. S., and P. A. Dykeman. 1982. *Edible Wild Plants: A North American Field Guide*. New York: Van Nostrand Reinhold.

Fenton, W. N. 1953. *The Iroquois Eagle Dance, an Offshoot of the Calumet Dance*. Bureau of American Ethnology Bulletin 156. Washington, D.C.: U.S. Government Printing Office.

Fenton, W. N. 1978. Northern Iroquoian Culture Patterns. In *Handbook of North American Indians, Vol. 15: Northeast*, ed. B. G. Trigger, pp. 296–321. Washington: Smithsonian Institution.

Filios, E. L. 1989. The End of the Beginning or the Beginning of the End: The Third Millennium B.P. in Southern New England. *Man in the Northeast* 38:79–93.

Finch, J. K. 1909. Aboriginal Remains on Manhattan Island. In *The Indians of Greater New York and the Lower Hudson*, ed. C. Wissler, pp. 64–73. *Anthropological Papers of the American Museum of Natural History*, Vol. III. New York: Hudson-Fulton.

Flanagan, D. 1975. Best Friend. *Scientific American* 233:50, 54.

Fowler, W. S. 1956. Sweet-Meadow Brook: A Pottery Site in Rhode Island. *Bulletin of the Massachusetts Archaeological Society* 18(1):1–23.

Fridman, E. J. N. 1989. *Of Domestication, Dog-Husbands and Dog-Feasts: Human-Canine Interaction in Native North America*. M.A. Thesis, Extension Studies, Harvard University, Boston.

George, D.R. 1993. Final Report on the Analysis of Faunal Material Recovered from Archaeological Investigations of a Woodland Period Component at the Lambert Farm Site, Warwick, Rhode Island (Appendix C). In Kerber 1994a:167–83.

Gero, J. M., and M. W. Conkey (eds.). 1991. *Engendering Archaeology: Women and Prehistory*. Oxford: Basil Blackwell.

Glassow, M. A. 1996. *Purisimeño Chumash Prehistory: Maritime Adaptations along the Southern California Coast*. Case Studies in Archaeology. New York: Harcourt Brace.

Goodby, R. G. 1992. Diversity as a Typological Construct: Understanding Late Woodland Ceramics from Narragansett Bay. Paper presented at the 32nd Annual Meeting of the Northeastern Anthropological Association, Bridgewater, Massachusetts.

Goodby, R. G. 1993. Native American Ceramics from the Lambert Farm Site (RI-269) (Appendix A). In Kerber 1994a:144–55.

Gowlett, J.A.J., R.E.M. Hedges, I.A. Law, and C. Perry. 1987. Radiocarbon Dates from the Oxford AMS System: Archaeometry Datelist 5. *Archaeometry* 29:125–55.

Gravier, J. 1694. Letter by Father Jacques Gravier in the Form of a Journal of the Mission of l'Immaculeé Conception de Notre Dame in the Ilinois Country. In Thwaites, ed. 1900, 64:158–237.

Grayson, D.K. 1988. Danger Cave, Last Supper Cave, and Hanging Rock Shelter: The Faunas. *Anthropological Papers of the American Museum of Natural History* 66(1).

Greenspan, R. L. 1990. The Rhode Island Sea Grant College Program Completion Report: Determination of Seasonality on *Mercenaria mercenaria* Shells from Archaeological Sites on Narragansett Bay, Rhode Island (Appendix D). In Kerber 1994a:184–93.

Greenspan, R. L. 1993. Dog Burial: Lambert Farm Site (Appendix B). In Kerber 1994a:156–66.

Guernsey, S. J., and A. V. Kidder. 1921. Basketmaker Caves of Northeastern Arizona. *Papers of the Peabody Museum of Archaeology and Ethnology* 8(2). Harvard University.

Guthrie, R. D. 1990. New Dates on Alaskan Quaternary Dogs and Wolves. *Current Research in the Pleistocene* 7:109–10.

Haag, W. G. 1948. An Osteometric Analysis of Some Aboriginal Dogs. *Reports in Anthropology* 7(3):107–264. University of Kentucky, Lexington.

Haigh, J. G. B., and M. A. Kelly. 1987. Contouring Techniques for Archaeological Distributions. *Journal of Archaeological Science* 14:231–41.

Hamilton, W. J., Jr., and J. O. Whitaker, Jr. 1979. *Mammals of the Eastern United States*. Ithaca, New York: Cornell University Press.

Hancock, M. E. 1984. Analysis of Shellfish Remains: Seasonality Information. In *Chapters in the Archeology of Cape Cod, I, Vol. 2*, ed. F.P. McManamon, pp. 121–56. Cultural Resources Management Study No. 8. National Park Service, Division of Cultural Resources, North Atlantic Region, Boston.

Handley, B.M. 1996. Role of the Shark in Southern New England Prehistory: Deity or Dinner? *Bulletin of the Massachusetts Archaeological Society* 57(1):27–34.

Harrington, M. 1982 [1900]. Exploration of an Ancient Burial Ground and Village Site near Port Washington, Long Island. In *The Second Coastal Archaeology Reader: 1900 to the Present*, ed. J. E. Truex, pp. 83–89. Readings in Long Island Archaeology and Ethnohistory Vol. V. Stony Brook: Suffolk County Archaeological Association.

Haury, E. W. 1950. *The Stratigraphy and Archaeology of Ventana Cave, Arizona*. Tucson and Albuquerque: University of Arizona Press and University of New Mexico Press.

Hayden, B. 1990. Nimrods, Piscators, Pluckers, and Planters: The Emergence of Food Production. *Journal of Anthropological Archaeology* 9:31–69.

Hayden, B. 1995. *The Pithouses of Keatley Creek: Complex Hunter/Gatherers of the Northwest Plateau*. Case Studies in Archaeology. In preparation.

Hill, F. C. 1972. *A Middle Archaic Dog Burial in Illinois*. Evanston: Foundation for Illinois Archaeology.

Hoffman, C. 1982. Plow Zones and Predictability: Sesquinary Context in New England Prehistoric Sites. *North American Archaeologist* 3(4):287–309.

Hoffman, C. 1983. Radiocarbon and Reality: The Fifth Millennium B.P. in Southern New England. *Man in the Northeast* 26:33–53.

Hunter, J. 1787. Observations Tending to Show That the Wolf, Jackal, and Dog Are All of the Same Species. *Philosophical Transactions of the Royal Society* of *London*.

Jeune, P. le. 1634a. Relation of What Occurred in New France in the Year 1634. In Thwaites, ed. 1897, 7:5–235.

Jeune, P. le. 1634b. Relation of What Occurred in New France in the Year 1634. In Thwaites, ed. 1897, 6:91–317.

Jeune, P. le. 1636. Relation of What Occurred in New France in the Year 1636. In Thwaites, ed. 1897, 8:7–197.

Jones, R. 1978. Why Did the Tasmanians Stop Eating Fish? In *Explorations in Ethnoarchaeology*, ed. R. A. Gould, pp. 11–48. Santa Fe: University of New Mexico Press.

Josselyn, J. 1988 [1674]. John Josselyn, Colonial Traveler: A Critical Edition of *Two Voyages to New-England*, ed. P. J. Lindholt. New Hampshire: University Press of New England.

Juli, H., and K. A. McBride. 1984. The Early and Middle Woodland Periods of Connecticut Prehistory: Focus on the Lower Connecticut River Valley. *Bulletin of the Archaeological Society of Connecticut* 47:89–98.

Kaeser, E. J. 1970. The Archery Range Site Ossuary, Pelham Bay Park, Bronx County, New York. *Pennsylvania Archaeologist* 40(1–2):9–34.

Kennish, M. J. 1980. Shell Microgrowth Analysis: *Mercenaria mercenaria* as a Type Example for Research in Population Dynamics. In *Skeletal Growth of Aquatic Organisms*, ed. D. C. Rhoads and R. A. Lutz, pp. 255–94. New York: Plenum Press.

Kerber, J. E. 1984. *Prehistoric Human Occupation and Changing Environment of Potowomut Neck, Warwick, Rhode Island: An Interdisciplinary Approach*. Ph.D. Dissertation, Anthropology, Brown University. Ann Arbor, University Microfilms.

Kerber, J. E. 1985. Digging for Clams: Shell Midden Analysis in New England. *North American Archaeologist* 6(2):97–113.

Kerber, J. E. 1994a. *Archaeological Investigations at the Lambert Farm Site, Warwick, Rhode Island: An Integrated Program of Research and Education by the Public Archaeology Laboratory, Inc. Vol. I*. The Public Archaeology Laboratory, Inc., Pawtucket, Rhode Island. Submitted to the Rhode Island Historical Preservation Commission, Providence.

Kerber, J. E. 1994b. Archaeological Research, Public Education, and Cultural Resource Management in the Northeast: An Integrative Approach. In *Cultural Resource Management: Archaeological Research, Preservation Planning, and Public Education in the Northeastern United States*, ed. J. E. Kerber, pp. 261–71. Connecticut: Bergin & Garvey.

Kerber, J. E. (ed.). 1984. *Prehistoric Human Occupation of Potowomut Neck: Brown University Field Methods Project*. Submitted to the Rhode Island Historical Preservation Commission, Providence.

Kerber, J. E., A. D. Leveillee, and R. L. Greenspan. 1989. An Unusual Dog Burial Feature at the Lambert Farm Site, Warwick, Rhode Island: Preliminary Observations. *Archaeology of Eastern North America* 17:165–74.

Krakker, J. J., M. J. Shott, and P. D. Welch. 1983. Design and Evaluation of Shovel Test Sampling in Regional Archaeological Survey. *Journal of Field Archaeology* 10:469–80.

Laet, J. de. 1909. New World, 1625, 1630, 1633, 1640. In *Narratives of New Netherland, 1609–1664*, ed. J. F. Jameson, pp. 29–60. New York: Charles Scribner's Sons.

Lalemant, J. (Hierosme). 1639. Relation of What Occurred in New France in the Year 1639. In Thwaites, ed. 1898, 17:7–215.

Lalemant, J. (Hierosme). 1642. Relation of What Occurred in New France in the Year 1642. In Thwaites, ed. 1898, 23:17–233.

Lalemant, J. (Hierosme). 1647. Relation of What Occurred in New France in the Year 1647. In Thwaites, ed. 1898, 32:17–55.

Largy, T. 1989. Analysis of Archeobotanical Samples from the Hoskins Park Site, the Lambert Farm Site, and Cedar Swamp. Ms. on file, the Public Archaeology Laboratory, Inc., Pawtucket, Rhode Island.

Largy, T. 1994. Archaeobotanical Analysis of the Lambert Farm Site (Appendix E). In Kerber 1994a:194–223.

Lawrence, B. 1967. Early Domestic Dogs. *Zeitschrift für Saugetierkunde* 32(1):44–59.

Leach, E. R. 1964. Anthropological Aspects of Language: Animal Categories and Verbal Abuse. In *New Directions in the Study of Language*, ed. E. H. Lenneberg, pp. 23–63. Cambridge: MIT Press.

Lescarbot, M. 1914. *The History of New France*. 3 Vols. Tran. by W. L. Grant. Toronto: The Champlain Society.

Lewis, T. N., and M. K. Lewis. 1961. *Eva, An Archaic Site*. Knoxville: University of Tennessee Press.

Lightfoot, K. G., and R. M. Cerrato. 1988. Prehistoric Shellfish Exploitation in Coastal New York. *Journal of Field Archaeology* 15:141–50.

Lightfoot, K. G., and R. M. Cerrato. 1989. Regional Patterns of Clam Harvesting along the Atlantic Coast of North America. *Archaeology of Eastern North America* 17:31–46.

Lopez, J., and S. Wisniewski. 1958. Discovery of a Possible Ceremonial Dog Burial in the City of Greater New York. *Bulletin of the Archaeological Society of Connecticut* 29:14–19.

Luedtke, B. E. 1980. The Calf Island Site and the Late Prehistoric Period in Boston Harbor. *Man in the Northeast* 20:25–76.

Lurker, M. 1974. *The Gods and Symbols of Ancient Egypt*. London: Thames and Hudson.

Marest, G. 1712. Letter from Father Gabriel Marest, Missionary of the Society of Jesus, to Father Germon, of the Same Society. In Thwaites, ed. 1900, 66:218–95.

McLoughlin, J. C. 1983. *The Canine Clan: A New Look at Man's Best Friend*. New York: The Viking Press.

McManamon, F. P. 1982. Prehistoric Land Use on Outer Cape Cod. *Journal of Field Archaeology* 9:1–20.

McMillan, R. B. 1970. Early Canid Burial from Western Ozark Highland. *Science* 167(3922):1246–47.

McPherron, A. L. 1966. *The Juntunen Site and the Late Woodland Prehistory of the Upper Great Lakes Area*. Ph.D. Dissertation, Anthropology, University of Michigan.

Mercier, F. le. 1637a. Relation of What Occurred in the Mission of the Society of Jesus, in the Land of the Hurons, in the Year 1637. In Thwaites, ed. 1898, 14:5–111.

Mercier, F. le. 1637b. Relation of What Occurred in the Mission of the Society of Jesus, in the Land of the Hurons, in the Year 1637. In Thwaites, ed. 1898, 13:5–267.

Miller, M. E., G. C. Christensen, and H. E. Evans. 1964. *Anatomy of the Dog*. Philadelphia: W. B. Saunders.

Morenon, E. P. 1981. *Archaeological Resources in an Urban Setting: The Warwick, Rhode Island Case Study, Vol. 2: Technical Data*. Papers in Archaeology No. 5. Public Archaeology Program. Rhode Island College, Providence.

Morey, D. F. 1992. Size, Shape and Development in the Evolution of the Domestic Dog. *Journal of Archaeological Science* 19:181–204.

Morey, D.F., and M.D. Wiant. 1992. Early Holocene Domestic Dog Burials from the North American Midwest. *Current Anthropology* 33(2):224–29.

Morgan, L. H. 1851. *League of the Ho-de-no-sau-nee, Iroquois*. Rochester: Sage and Brothers.

Nelson, C. M. 1989. Radiocarbon Age of the Dog Burial from Squantum, Massachusetts. *Massachusetts Archaeological Society Bulletin* 50(1):29.

Newman, W. S. 1974. A Comment on Snow's 'Rising Sea Level and Prehistoric Cultural Chronology in Northern New England.' *American Antiquity* 39:135–36.

Olsen, J. W. 1985. Prehistoric Dogs in Mainland East Asia (Chapter 5). In S. J. Olsen 1985:47–70.

Olsen, S. J. 1979. Archaeologically, What Constitutes an Early Domestic Animal? In *Advances in Archaeological Method and Theory*, Vol. 2, ed. M. B. Schiffer, pp. 175–97. New York: Academic Press.

Olsen, S. J. 1985. *Origins of the Domestic Dog*. Tucson: University of Arizona Press.

Olsen, S. J., and J. W. Olsen. 1977. The Chinese Wolf, Ancestor of New World Dogs. *Science* 197(4303):533–35.

Orchard, F. P. 1977 [1928]. A Matinecoc Site on Long Island. In *Early Papers in Long Island Archaeology*, ed. G. Levine, pp. 66–69. Readings in Long Island Archaeology and Ethnohistory Vol. I. Stony Brook: Suffolk County Archaeological Association.

Peet, T. E. 1914. *The Cemeteries of Abydos, Part II—1911–1912*. Memoir 34. London: The Egypt Exploration Fund.

Pferd, W., III. 1987. *Dogs of the American Indians*. Virginia: Denlinger's Publishers, Ltd.

Prahl, E. J. 1967. Prehistoric Dogs of Michigan. *Michigan Archaeologist* 13(1):13–27.

Pring, M. 1906. A Voyage Set Out from the Citie of Bristoll. In *Early English and French Voyages, 1534–1608*, ed. H. S. Burrage, pp. 341 52. New York: Charles Scribner's Sons.

Quilter, J., and T. Stocker. 1983. Subsistence Economies and the Origins of Andean Complex Societies. *American Anthropologist* 85(3):545–62.

Redman, C., and P. J. Watson. 1970. Systematic Intensive Surface Collection. *American Antiquity* 35(3):279–91.

Ritchie, W. A. 1945. *An Early Site in Cayuga County, New York: Type Component of the Frontenac Focus.* Researches and Transactions of the New York State Archeological Association 10. Research Records of the Rochester Museum of Arts and Sciences 7.

Ritchie, W. A. 1959. *The Stony Brook Site and its Relation to Archaic and Transitional Cultures on Long Island.* New York State Museum and Science Service Bulletin 372. Albany.

Ritchie, W. A. 1969. *The Archaeology of Martha's Vineyard.* New Jersey: Natural History Press.

Ritchie, W. A. 1971. *A Typology and Nomenclature for New York Projectile Points.* Rev. ed. New York State Museum and Science Service Bulletin 384. Albany, New York: SUNY State Education Department.

Ritchie, W. A. 1980. *The Archaeology of New York State.* Rev. ed. Harrison, N.Y.: Harbor Hill Books.

Rogers, E. H. 1943. The Indian River Village Site. *Bulletin of the Archaeological Society of Connecticut* 14.

Roper, D. C. 1976. Lateral Displacement of Artifacts Due to Plowing. *American Antiquity* 41(3):372–75.

Sagard, G. 1939. *The Long Journey to the Country of the Hurons*, ed. G. M. Wrong, tran. H. H. Langton. Toronto: The Champlain Society.

Sargent, H. 1952. A Preliminary Report on the Excavations at Grannis Island. *Bulletin of the Archaeological Society of Connecticut* 26:30–50.

Simmons, W. S. 1978. Narragansett. In *Handbook of North American Indians, Vol. 15: Northeast*, ed. B.G. Trigger, pp. 190–97. Washington: Smithsonian Institution.

Skinner, A. 1909. Archaeology of the Coastal New York Algonkin. In *The Indians of Greater New York and the Lower Hudson*, ed. C. Wissler, pp. 211–35. *Anthropological Papers of the American Museum of Natural History*, Vol. III. New York: Hudson-Fulton.

Smith, C. H. 1839. Dogs. In *The Naturalist's Library Series, Mammalia*, ed. W. J. Bart, Vol. IX. Edinburgh.

Snow, D. R. 1972. Rising Sea Level and Prehistoric Cultural Ecology in Northern New England. *American Antiquity* 37:211–22.

Speck, F. G. 1925. Dogs of the Labrador Indians. *Natural History* 25:58–64.

Spector, J. D., and M. K. Whelan. 1989. Incorporating Gender into Archaeology Courses. In *Gender and Anthropology: Critical Reviews for Research and Teaching*, ed. S. Morgen, pp. 65–94. Washington, D.C.: American Anthropological Association.

Spiess, A. E., and R. A. Lewis. 1995. Features and Activity Areas: The Spatial Analysis of Faunal Remains (Appendix 8). In Bourque 1995:337–73.

Sterud, E., F. P. McManamon, and M. Rose. 1978. The Identification of Activity Loci in Ploughzones: An Example from New York State. *Man in the Northeast* 15–16:94–117.

Strong, J. A. 1985. Late Woodland Dog Ceremonialism on Long Island in Comparative and Temporal Perspective. *The Bulletin and Journal of the New York State Archaeological Association* 91:32–38.

Struever, S., and F. A. Holton. 1979. *Koster: Americans in Search of Their Prehistoric Past.* New York: Anchor Press/Doubleday.

Stuiver, M., and T. F. Braziunas. 1993. Modeling Atmospheric ^{14}C Influences and Radiocarbon Ages of Marine Samples Back to 10,000 B.C. *Radiocarbon* 35:137–89.

Stuiver, M., and G. W. Pearson. 1993. High-Precision Bidecadal Calibration of the Radiocarbon Time Scale, A.D. 1950–500 B.C. and 2500–6000 B.C. *Radiocarbon* 35:1–23.

Stuiver, M., and P. J. Reimer. 1993a. Extended ¹⁴C Data Base and Revised Calib 3.0 ¹⁴C Age Calibration Program. *Radiocarbon* 35:215–30.

Stuiver, M., and P. J. Reimer. 1993b. CALIB User's Guide Rev 3.0.3. Quaternary Isotope Laboratory, University of Washington, Seattle.

Tantaquidgeon, G. 1942. *A Study of Delaware Indian Medicine Practice and Folk Beliefs*. Harrisburg: Pennsylvania Historical Commission.

Thorbahn, P. F., and D. C. Cox. 1988. The Effect of Estuary Formation on Prehistoric Settlement in Southern Rhode Island. In *Holocene Human Ecology in Northeastern North America*, ed. G. P. Nicholas, pp. 167–82. New York: Plenum Press.

Thwaites, R. G. 1896. Historical Introduction. In Thwaites, ed. 1896, 1:1–44.

Thwaites, R. G. (ed.). 1896–1901. *The Jesuit Relations and Allied Documents: Travels and Explorations of Jesuit Missionaries in New France, 1610–1791*. (73 vols.). Cleveland: The Burrows Brothers.

Tooker, E. 1970. *The Iroquois Ceremonial of Midwinter*. Syracuse: Syracuse University Press.

Trubowitz, N. L. 1978. The Persistence of Settlement in a Cultivated Field. In *Essays in Memory of Marian E. White*, ed. W. E. Engelbrecht and D. K. Grayson, pp. 41–66. Occasional Publications in Northeastern Anthropology. Rindge, New Hampshire.

Tuck, J. A. 1970. An Archaic Indian Cemetery in Newfoundland. *Scientific American* 222(6):112–21.

Turnbull, P. F., and C. A. Reed. 1974. The Fauna from the Terminal Pleistocene of Palegawra Cave, a Zarzian Occupation Site in North-Eastern Iraq. *Fieldiana Anthropology*, Field Museum of Natural History 63(3):81–146.

Walker, D. N., and G. C. Frison. 1982. Studies on Amerind Dogs, 3: Prehistoric Wolf/Dog Hybrids from the Northwestern Plains. *Journal of Archaeological Science* 9:125–72.

Wapnish, P., and B. Hesse. 1993. Pampered Pooches or Plain Pariahs? The Ashkelon Dog Burials. *Biblical Archaeologist* 56(2):55–80.

Wassenaer, N. van. 1909. Historisch Verhael, 1624–1630. In *Narratives of New Netherland, 1609–1664*, ed. J. F. Jameson, pp. 61–96. New York: Charles Scribner's Sons.

Watson, P. J. 1976. In Pursuit of Prehistoric Subsistence: A Comparative Account of Some Contemporary Flotation Techniques. *Midcontinental Journal of Archaeology* 1:77–100.

Webb, W. S. 1974. *Indian Knoll*. Rev. ed. Knoxville: University of Tennessee Press.

Whalen, M. 1985. A Rapid Technique for Three-Dimensional Site Mapping. *North American Archaeologist* 6:193–211.

Williams, R. 1973 [1643]. *A Key into the Language of America*, ed. J. J. Teunissen and E. J. Hinz. Detroit: Wayne State University Press.

Wing, E. 1977. Animal Domestication in the Andes. In *Origins of Agriculture*, ed. C. A. Reed, pp. 837–59. The Hague, Paris: Mouton.

Wood, W. 1977 [1634]. *New England's Prospect*, ed. A. T. Vaughan. Amherst: University of Massachusetts Press.

Wroth, L. C. 1970. *The Voyages of Giovanni da Verrazzano, 1524–1528*. New Haven: Yale University Press.

Wyman, J. 1868. An Account of Some Kjockkenmoeddings, or Shell Heaps, in Maine and Massachusetts. *American Naturalist* I:561–84.

Zeisberger, D. 1910. History of the Northern American Indians. In *Ohio State Archaeological and Historical Quarterly* 19:1–189, ed. A. B. Hulbert and W. N. Schwarze. Columbus: Fred J. Heer.

Credits

Figure 4.3   Alan Leveillee (Public Archaeology Laboratory, Inc.)

Figure 4.9   Mary Lynn Rainey (Public Archaeology Laboratory, Inc.)

Figures 5.1, 5.5   *Origins of the Domestic
Dog: The Fossil Record,* Stanley J. Olsen,
University of Arizona Press (1985)

Figure 5.3   Negatives/Transparencies
#335567; Courtesy of the Department of
Library Services, American Museum of
Natural History

Figure 5.4   Michael Wiant (Center for
American Archaeology)

Figures 1.1, 1.2, 1.3, 2.4, and 5.2   Prepared by Christine Rossi

Figures 3.2, 3.3, 3.4, 4.1, 4.2, and 4.8
Prepared by Laura Thode

Figure 4.4   Prepared by Imogene Lim

Index

Abenaki Indians, 1, 97
Abydos site, 82, 85
Adzes, 4, 39
Agate Basin site, 82, 83
Airport site, 50
Allen, G. M., 80
Animal remains. *See* Dogs; Faunal remains
   (non-dog); Shell deposits
Anyang Archaeological Team (Institute of
   Archaeology, Chinese Academy of
   Social Sciences), 86
Archaic period, 3, 5, 6, 33, 34, 37, 52, 77,
   86, 88, 89, 90, 92, 94, 98
Archery Range site, 2, 92
Artifacts. *See specific artifact types, such
   as* Projectile points
Ashkelon site, 82, 85–86
Assiniboin Indians, 84, 96
Axes, 4, 39, 63, 64

Barber, R. J., 62
Barton, B. S., 80
Beach Haven site, 93
Bernabo, J. C., 59
Bernstein, D. J., 37, 59, 60, 62
Biard, P., 98, 99
Bifaces (non-projectile points), 35, 38, 39,
   40, 50
Blick, J. P., 92
Blukis Onat, A. R., 77
Bolton, R. P., 93, 104
Bone artifacts, 63, 65
Bones. *See* Dogs; Faunal remains (non-
   dog); Human burials, with dog
   remains
Bourque, B. J., 98
Braun, D. P., 7
Braziunas, T. F., 32

Brébeuf, J. de, 97
Brizinski, M., 91
Burials. *See* Dogs; Human burials, with
   dog remains
Butler, E., 99

Calf Island site, 2, 55
Calver, W. L., 93, 104
Campbell site, 59
Canids (Canidae family), members of, 79
Canines. *See Canis* genus, members of;
   Canids, members of; Dogs; Wolves
Canis genus, members of, 79
Cantwell, A. M., 90, 91, 92, 103
Cardozo, C., 84
Cartier, J., 95
Cayuga Indians, 1, 101
Ceci, L., 59
Ceramics (prehistoric), 6, 23, 24, 29, 33,
   34–36, 37, 42, 43, 44, 46, 47–49, 52,
   55, 63, 67, 73, 92, 106
Cerrato, R. M., 62
Champlain, S., 95
Chapin, H. M., 101
Charcoal, 29, 52, 66, 67, 73, 83, 86, 98,
   101
Cheever, G. B., 96
Chipped-stone tools. *See specific chipped-
   stone tool types, such as* Projectile
   points
Chippewa Indians, 58
Chipping debris, 4, 6, 23, 30, 38, 39–42,
   43, 44, 51, 55, 63, 66, 67, 73, 94, 106
   See also Worked flakes
Claassen, C., 77
Clutton-Brock, J., 80, 83
Coastal archaeology, 4–7
College Point site, 2, 91

Colton, H. S., 88
Conkey, M. W., 4
Conservation archaeology, 18–19
    See also Cultural resource management
Conservation ethic, 14, 18–19
Cores (stone), 39, 40, 41
Cotuit Port site, 54
Cox, D. C., 59
Crellin, D. F., 96
Crépieul, F. de, 97
CRM. *See* Cultural resource management
Cronan, J. M., 60
Cultural resource management (CRM).
    See also Conservation archaeology
    developers and, 9–11, 107
    legislation and, 1, 9–11, 18
    public education and, 11–14, 15, 16, 17

Dablon, C., 99
Danger Cave site, 83
Darwin C., 80
Davis, S. J. M., 85
DeForest, J. W., 61
Degerbøl, M., 82
Delaware Indians, 1, 96, 101
Densmore, F., 58
Denys, N., 96, 97, 100
Dogs *(Canis familiaris)*
    burials of, 54, 84–94, 98, 103, 104
    burials of from Lambert Farm site (*see*
        Lambert Farm site, dog burials from)
    disarticulated remains of, 54, 55, 80,
        81–83, 91, 94, 98, 99–100
    disarticulated remains of from Lambert
        Farm site (*see* Lambert Farm site,
        disarticulated dog remains from)
    domestication of, 80–83
    ethnohistorical observations of, 7, 78,
        79, 83, 84, 94–101, 103, 104, 105
    mummified remains of, 88, 89
    origins of, 79–83
Donahue, D. J., 32
Drake, S. G., 99
Drills, 34, 39, 40, 63
Dykeman, P. A., 58

Eagle Hill site, 54
Early Archaic period, 5, 86, 92

Early Woodland period, 33, 34, 36, 37
Eaton, G. F., 54
Ein Mallaha (Eynan) site, 82, 85
Elias, T. S., 58
Eva site, 82, 88
Excavation. *See* Features, general
    excavation techniques of; Excavation
    Units, general excavation techniques
    of; Lambert Farm site, sampling of;
    Shovel Test Pits, general excavation
    techniques of; Unusual sample units,
    general excavation techniques of
Excavation Units (EUs), general
    excavation techniques of, 24–25

Fairbanks Creek site, 82, 83
Faunal remains (dog). *See* Dogs
Faunal remains (non-dog), 1, 5, 6–7, 25,
    26–28, 51, 52, 53–55, 59–62, 63–78,
    87, 91, 93–94, 97, 98, 104
    See also Shell deposits
Features
    defined, 20
    Feature 2, 26–27, 51, 55, 58, 60, 62, 63,
        65–72, 74, 76–78
    Feature 22, 26–27, 31, 51, 58, 60, 62,
        63, 65–66, 68–69, 71–78
    general excavation techniques of, 24–25
Fenton, W. N., 99
Fieldwork. *See* Excavation
Filios, E. L., 37
Finch, J. K., 93, 104
Fire-cracked rocks, 67
Flakes. *See* Chipping debris; Worked
    flakes
Flanagan, D., 82
Floral remains, 3, 5, 6, 51, 53, 55–59, 60,
    61, 62, 63, 77, 105, 106
Flotation, 38, 55, 56–57, 58, 59, 62
Fowler, W. S., 94
Frank Bay site, 2, 91
Fridman, E. J. N., 96, 101
Frison, G. C., 83
Frontenac Island site, 2, 90

Gaming stone, 39, 63, 64
George, D. R., 53, 54, 55, 60, 61, 62, 63, 77

Gero, J. M., 4
Glaciation, 4–5, 9, 24, 83
Glassow, M. A., 25
Goodby, R. G., 34–35, 36
Gowlett, J. A., 83
Grannis Island site, 2, 93
Graphite objects, 39, 40, 63
Grasshopper Pueblo site, 82, 83–84
Gravier, J., 99
Grayson, D. K., 83
Greenspan, R. L., 60, 76–77
Greenwich Cove site, 8, 59, 60, 62
Groundstone tools. *See specific ground-
stone tool types, such as* Axes
Guernsey, S. J., 88
Guthrie, R. D., 83

Haag, W. G., 80, 85
Hadlock, W. S., 99
Haigh, J. G. B., 48
Hamilton, W. J., Jr., 60, 61
Hammerstones, 38, 39, 42, 63
Hancock, M. E., 62
Handley, B. M., 64–65
Harrington, M., 92–93
Hatch site. *See* Weyanoke Old Town site
Haury, E. W., 88
Hayden, B., 96, 99–100
Hesse, B., 80, 85
Hill, F. C., 87
Historic Preservation. *See* Cultural
resource management
Historic remains, 3, 4, 30, 38, 58, 66,
85–86
Hoffman, C., 37, 50
Holton, F. A., 86
Human burials, with dog remains, 54, 85,
86, 88–94, 99, 103, 105
Human prehistory
defined, 2–3
limitations in interpreting, 3–4, 5, 23,
25, 37–38, 42, 43, 45–51, 60, 62
Hunter, J., 80
Huron Indians, 1, 95, 97, 99, 100

Indian Knoll site, 82, 88
Indians. *See names of specific tribes*

Iroquois Indians, 1, 3, 97, 99, 100–101, 104
See also Cayuga Indians; Mohawk
Indians; Oneida Indians; Onondaga
Indians; Seneca Indians

Jaguar Cave site, 82, 83, 87
Jeune, P. le, 97, 101
Jones, R., 7
Josselyn, J., 61, 96
Juli, H., 37
Juntunen site, 2, 91

Kaeser, E. J., 91, 92
Keatley Creek site, 82, 96, 99
Kelly, M. A., 48
Kennish, M. J., 60
Kerber, J. E., 13, 14, 37, 62, 76, 94
Kidder, A. V., 88
Koster site, 82, 86–88
Krakker, J. J., 21

Laet, J. de, 96
Lake Montauk site, 2, 93
Lalemant, J. (Hierosme), 97, 99, 100
Lambert Farm site
disarticulated dog remains from, 7, 53,
76–77, 104–105
discovery of, 9
disturbances to, 23, 25, 42, 43, 45–46,
50–51, 53, 104
dog burials from, 1, 7, 26–27, 53,
66–78, 94, 104, 105, 107
human skeletal remains from, 65, 105
laboratory processing of remains from,
15, 16, 29–31, 55, 60
location of, 1, 2, 8–9, 10
prehistoric periods of use of, 32–38, 105
prehistoric subsistence at, 7, 25, 26–27,
51, 52–54, 55, 56–57, 58–59, 60–62,
63–75, 77–78, 104, 105, 106
public archaeology at, 11–14, 15–18,
26–31, 107
radiocarbon dating of remains from, 25,
31–33, 37–38, 51, 77, 78, 107
residential development of, 10–13, 15,
18, 20, 21, 26, 27, 38, 50, 68, 106

Lambert Farm site *(continued)*
  sampling of, 12, 15–26, 28
  seasonality reconstructions of prehistoric
    remains from, 51, 53, 55, 59–62, 78
  spatial patterning of prehistoric remains
    from, 20, 38, 42, 43–51, 67
Largy, T., 56–57, 58, 62
Late Archaic period, 33, 52, 88, 94, 98
Late Woodland period, 33, 35, 36, 37, 38,
    52, 55, 92, 94, 105, 106
Latham R., 93
Lawrence, B., 82, 83
Leach, E. R., 103
Lescarbot, M., 96
Leveillee, A. D., 11, 13, 26, 27
Lewis, M. K., 88
Lewis, R. A., 98
Lewis, T. N., 88
Lightfoot, K. G., 62
Lopez, J., 91
Luedtke, B. E., 55
Lurker, M., 85

Macera I site, 8, 52
Macera II site, 8, 52
Marest, G., 99
Maritime Archaic period (Moorehead
    phase), 89, 98
McBride, K. A., 37
McLoughlin, J. C., 79, 80
McManamon, F. P., 38, 41, 43, 50
McMillan, R. B., 88
McPherron, A. L., 91
Mercier, F. le, 97, 99, 100
Micmac Indians, 1, 96, 97, 98, 100
Middle Archaic period, 88
Middle Woodland period, 33, 34, 36, 37,
    90, 92
Miller, M. E., 76
Mohawk Indians, 1, 99, 101
Montagnais Indians, 97–98
Morenon, E. P., 9, 10, 16, 52, 94
Morey, D. F., 80, 83, 86–87
Morgan, L. H., 100–101

Narragansett Bay, 8, 36, 59, 60, 67, 77, 78,
    105

Narragansett Indians, 1, 101, 105, 106
Naskapi Indians, 97–98
Native Americans. *See names of specific*
    tribes
Nelson, C. M., 94
Newman, W. S., 7
Noe-Nygaard, N., 83
Northeastern North America, region of, 1, 2
Nutshells. *See* Floral remains

Olsen, J. W., 80, 82, 86, 88
Olsen, S. J., 79, 80, 81, 82, 83, 84, 88, 89
Oneida Indians, 1, 99, 101
Onondaga Indians, 1, 101
Orchard, F. P., 93
Ottawa Indians, 97

PAL. *See* Public Archaeology Laboratory
Palegawra Cave site, 81–82
Paleoindian period, 3, 5, 6, 83
Paloma site, 51–52, 82
Pan-p'o site, 82, 83
Pearson, G. W., 32
Peet, T. E., 85
Pequot Indians, 1
Pferd, W., III, 83, 88, 89–90, 95
Plant remains. *See* Floral remains
Port au Choix site, 2, 89, 90
Port Washington site, 2, 92–93
Pottery (prehistoric). *See* Ceramics
    (prehistoric)
Prahl, E. J., 91
Preforms, 35, 39, 40, 43
Prehistoric artifacts. *See specific*
    prehistoric artifact types, such as
    Projectile points
Prehistory. *See* Human prehistory
Pring, M., 96
Projectile points, 3, 4, 5, 23, 24, 33–34, 35,
    37, 38–39, 40, 42, 43, 44, 47, 48–49,
    63, 93
Public Archaeology Laboratory (PAL), 11,
    13, 16, 26, 27, 29, 30, 55, 60, 67, 68
Public education and archaeology. *See*
    Cultural resource management, public
    education and; Lambert Farm site,
    public archaeology at

Quartz crystals, 67, 69, 91
Quilter, J., 51, 52, 95

Radiocarbon dating
   defined, 31–32
   at Lambert Farm site (*see* Lambert Farm
      site, radiocarbon dating of remains
      from)
Raw Materials
   of chipping debris, 38, 39–40, 41, 67,
      73, 106
   of stone artifacts, 38–39, 40, 63, 106
Redman, C., 43, 50
Reed, C. A., 81
Reimer, P. J., 32
Research design, 14, 15, 29, 50
Rhode Island Historical Preservation
      Commission, 9, 11, 26, 31
RI-972 site, 8, 94
Ridge Camp site, 2, 91
Ritchie, W. A., 6–7, 33, 90
Robinson, P., 11, 26
Rodgers Shelter site, 82, 88
Rogers, E. H., 91
Roper, D. C., 50

Sagard, G., 100
Sampling. *See also* Excavation
   defined, 18–20
   at Lambert Farm site (*see* Lambert Farm
      site, sampling of)
Sargent, H., 94
Savage, H., 91
Scrapers, 4, 35, 39, 40, 63
Sea level changes, 4, 5–6, 8
Seeds. *See* Floral remains
Seneca Indians, 1, 100, 101
Shell deposits, 1, 4, 5, 6–7, 20, 23, 24, 25,
      26–28, 51, 52, 53, 60, 62, 63, 64,
      65–78, 87, 93–94, 98, 104
Shovel Test Pits (STPs), general excava-
      tion techniques of, 21, 22–24, 25
Simmons, W. S., 106
Skinner, A., 104
Smith, C. H., 80
Smoking pipes (prehistoric), 39, 64, 67,
      69, 77, 94

Snow, D. R., 6–7
Speck, F. G., 97–98
Spector, J. D., 4
Spiess, A. E., 98
Squantum site, 2, 94
Star Carr site, 82
Sterud, E., 43, 50
Stocker, T., 51, 52
Stone artifacts. *See specific stone artifact
      types, such as* Projectile points
Strong, J. A., 89, 92, 93, 103
Struever, S., 86
Stuiver, M., 32
Sweet-Meadow Brook site, 8, 94

Tamers, Murry, 32, 33
Tantaquidgeon, G., 101
Thompson, D., 93
Thorbahn, P. F., 59
Thwaites, R. G., 96–97
Tooker, E., 100, 101
Tools. *See specific tool types, such as*
      Projectile points
Transitional (Terminal) Archaic period, 33,
      34, 37, 90
Trubowitz, N. L., 50
Tuck, J. A., 89–90
Turnbull, P. F., 81
Turner Farm site, 2, 98

Unifaces, 39, 40
Untyped stone tools, 34, 35, 39
Unusual sample units (SFs and SUs),
      general excavation techniques of,
      27–28

Valla, F. R., 85
Ventana Cave site, 82, 88

Walker, D. N., 83
Wampanoag Indians, 1, 99
Wapnish, P., 80, 85
Wassenaer, N. van, 96
Watson, P. J., 43, 50, 55
Webb, W. S., 88

Weyanoke Old Town (Hatch) site, 2,
    91–92
Whalen, M., 21
Whelan, M. K., 4
Whitaker, J. O., Jr., 60, 61
White Dog Cave site, 82, 88, 89
Wiant, M. D., 83, 86–87
Williams, R., 1, 59, 61, 101, 106
Wing, E., 83
Wisniewski, S., 91
Wolves, 53, 54, 79, 80, 82–84, 85, 94, 95,
    96, 97
Wood, W., 61

Woodland period, 3, 5, 6, 7, 9, 33, 34, 35,
    36, 37, 38, 52, 55, 59, 62, 90, 91, 92,
    94, 105, 106
Worked flakes, 39, 40
Wroth, L. C., 59, 105
Wyman, J., 54

Yin site, 82, 86

Zeisberger, D., 96
Zhoukoudian site, 82